W9-AMU-835

Wild Truth Journal

pictures of God

50 life lessons from
the Scriptures for junior highers
& middle schoolers

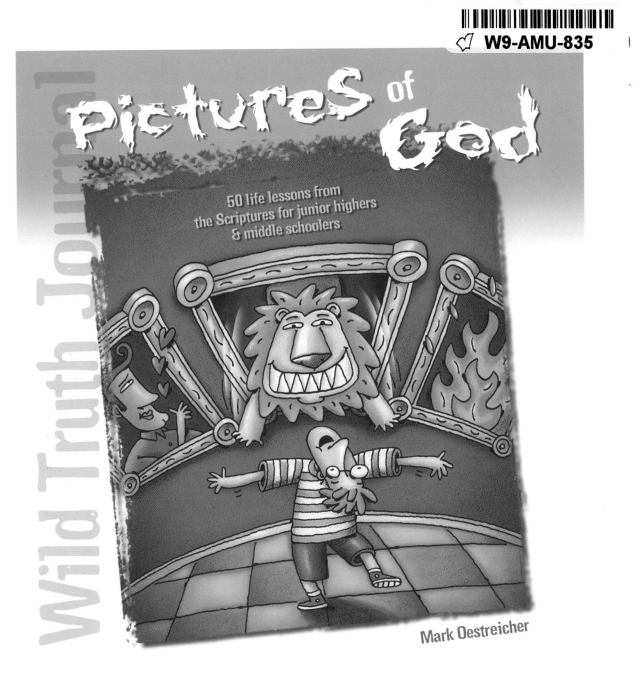

Mark Oestreicher

ZONDERVAN®

ZONDERVAN.com/
AUTHORTRACKER
follow your favorite authors

youth
specialties

**youth
specialties**

Wild Truth Journal—Pictures of God: 50 life lessons from the Scriptures for junior highers & middle schoolers
Copyright 2007 by Youth Specialties, Inc.

Youth Specialties resources, 300 S. Pierce St., El Cajon, CA 92020 are published by Zondervan, 5300 Patterson Ave. SE, Grand Rapids, MI 49530.

ISBN-10: 0-310-22350-4
ISBN-13: 978-0-310-22350-4

All Scripture quotations, unless otherwise indicated, are taken from the *Holy Bible, Today's New International Version*®. NIV®. Copyright 1973, 1978, 1984 by International Bible Society. Used by permission of Zondervan. All rights reserved.

All rights reserved. No part of this publication may be reproduced, stored in a retrieval system, or transmitted in any form or by any means — electronic, mechanical, photocopy, recording, or any other — except for brief quotations in printed reviews, without the prior permission of the publisher.

The original concept for this book, including the wording in some of the introductions, comes from *52 Ways to Teach Your Child About God,* written by Todd Temple and published by Oliver-Nelson Books, a division of Thomas Nelson, Inc., Publishers.

Cover design and Interior design by Patton Bros. Design
Cover and interior illustrations by Kreig Barrie

Printed in the United States of America

08 09 10 11 12 13 14 15 16 17 18 19 20 • 20 19 18 17 16 15 14 13 12 11 10 9 8

Contents

God is like a—

To my son, Max Turner Oestreicher.
May you grow up to know and love the God who is so amazing
that fifty pictures can only begin to describe him.

Thanks, as always, to my wonderful wife, Jeannie, for encouraging this writing ministry and to my daughter, Liesl, for not touching the keyboard while Daddy was typing. Thanks to the awesome staff in the product department of Youth Specialties for making my transition from author to coworker a true joy. Thanks to Todd Temple, the creator of the Wild Truth line and the outline of this book. And thanks to my God, for revealing himself in so many ways through Scripture and the world around us.

Stuff for your youth group leader to read

The inventor of junior highers—God himself—also happens to have invented the two best ways to communicate to them: pictures and people.

This book is all about *pictures*. Specifically, snapshots of God and his awesome character. It's written so students can examine these pictures for themselves, without any adult supervision whatsoever. (A scary thought, but pretty cool, too.) Each lesson opens with an *action shot*—a picture of God straight from the Bible. After examining the portrait, students are invited to *copy* it—to develop that same godly character trait in their own lives. The lesson ends with a call to action—to *print* what they've learned by applying it in an immediately practical way.

But the fact that these lessons work well on their own doesn't mean you can't use the book to support your group stuff. In fact, it makes for a great adventure in small group settings. Here's how—

Give each member of the group a copy of the journal, then agree with your students on the number of lessons they'll do each week. Hold them accountable to this commitment: Call and encourage them, let them know they're all in this together. (And by *together*, we mean, you do them too!) Set a time for the group to meet each week to discuss the just-completed lessons. For real growth, assign a different group member to lead the discussion on each lesson.

You can also use these self-portraits of God in your large group teaching. Tweak the questions, add your own illustrations and activities—whatever works best for your students. Or, better yet, get yourself a copy of *Wild Truth Bible Lessons—Pictures of God*. It's got 12 hot lessons based on a dozen of the God-portraits revealed in this journal.

This journal is the sequel to *Wild Truth Journal*, which capitalizes on God's other great truth-revealing invention—*people*. The original journal introduces your students to 50 amazing characters straight from the Bible and shows how God used them to demonstrate what it means to live for him. By the way, for engaging teaching resources on these characters, check out *Wild Truth Bible Lessons* and *Wild Truth Bible Lessons 2*. Each contains full-blown lessons on 12 of the characters found in *WTJ*.

One last thing. All the books I've cleverly pitched above are written by Mark Oestreicher, a friend and youth ministry cohort whose delightfully dangerous skill in communicating the Truth to junior highers is eclipsed only by his passion for their Inventor. So if you should find yourself using this journal for your *own* devotions...then, well, welcome to the club. I won't tell if you don't.

Todd Temple
10 TO 20

Stuff for you to read

Say "Cheese!"

Does your Bible have photos in it? Most don't. Just some maps in the back. Photography was developed *way* too late to catch God on film. That's too bad. Some of those Bible scenes would be pretty spectacular to look at. But God didn't give us any pictures of himself. Just a bunch of words.

Stop right there! God *did* give us pictures—but he used *words* to draw them. And it's a good thing he did. Because he's so absolutely gigantic, he could never fit into a photo. Not even with a wide-angle lens. But pictures made with words can be *as big as your imagination.*

To help us picture him in our heads, God uses word pictures we already know. When he says he's our *father*, we know what that looks like because we've seen fathers before. When Jesus says he's the bread of life, we know just what he means: he satisfies our hunger like fresh-baked bread in an empty stomach. The Bible is filled with great word pictures: sometimes they're huge portraits; sometimes they're little snapshots. But if you look close enough, you'll find a picture of God on just about every page.

But the Bible isn't like a *Where's Waldo* book. When you find God's picture, don't just say, "There he is!" and turn the page. Stop for a moment...take a closer look...picture him in your head. Then ask yourself: "What's God trying to show me in this picture?" Because when God puts his self-portrait on the page, he's showing you something very important about himself. *He's revealing a part of his* **character**.

You see, he wants you to know him better. To know what he's *really* like. To know in your head and heart who he is and how much he loves you. But wait. There's more: God wants you to **copy the picture!** Yep, he wants you to print *his* picture into *your* life. Not a cardboard cutout that you stand behind. But a real, true picture of him *in* your life. So that when people see your *character*, they'll say, "You remind me of someone, but I can't remember who." Then you can show them the Original. So they can copy God's character too.

This journal will help you do that. It's got 50 stunning pictures straight out of God's photo album—the Bible! Set aside time each week to do two or three picture-lessons. If you do, this book will last you half a year. Half a year of God's great self-portraits, suitable for framing into your own character. Start now!

God is like a
COMEDIAN

Our mouths were filled with laughter,
our tongues with songs of joy.   **Psalm 126:2**

This God-picture isn't one you hear about very often. It's easy to imagine God as an old guy who doesn't have any fun. But think again. We're talking about the God who made dogs chase their own tails...the God who made monkeys swing around in trees...the God who thought up burping and passing gas (he even gave it a sound!) Face it—God likes to have fun. And he wants us to laugh and have fun, too. After all, he invented laughter!

Action shot | **Read Job 8:21**

Close-up

What difference does it make to you that God likes laughter, fun, and humor?

Which of these do you think is the funniest animal?

- ☐ giant squid
- ☐ otter
- ☐ octopus
- ☐ prairie dog
- ☐ other:_____
- ☐ monkey
- ☐ pig
- ☐ kangaroo
- ☐ sloth

You are here

PENTATEUCH

OLD TESTAMENT

HISTORY — Esther / **JOB** / Psalms

POETRY

PROPHECY

NEW TESTAMENT

HISTORY

LETTERS

PROPHECY

God's got a sense of humor, and he put it in you, too! Write about something funny that happened to you recently (or make up a funny story).

What kinds of things make you laugh the most? Rank these from most funny (1) to least funny (8).

____ a good joke

____ watching a funny movie

____ a friend laughing real hard

____ a funny song

____ slapstick (physical humor)

____ this TV show: _____

____ being tickled

____ a funny real-life story

Okay, tough question here: How can you use humor and laughter in a good way, in a way that honors God?

Print it!

Use humor to lift someone's spirit this week. Write the name of someone who could use a dose of humor: _____

How will you give this person that dose?

❑ tell a joke

❑ play a funny song

❑ cut out a funny cartoon

❑ rent a funny movie and watch it together

❑ share a funny story or article

❑ other:_____

God is like a
GENiUS

Among all the wise men of the nations and in all their kingdoms, there is no one like you. *Jeremiah 10:7*

He knows all your problems, including the ones you won't admit to (and a dozen more you don't even know you have). God the Genius knows about your biggest dreams, your worst fears. He's the only one who knows that you still check under your bed for the bogeyman. He knows the best answer to your toughest dilemmas.

And what's even more amazing than how much he knows? How little we ask him for the answers. Look at it this way: here's this guy who knows *everything*, and most of us don't even bother to ask him for advice. He has been known to share his knowledge with those who want it, you know.

ction shot | **Read Psalm 147:5**

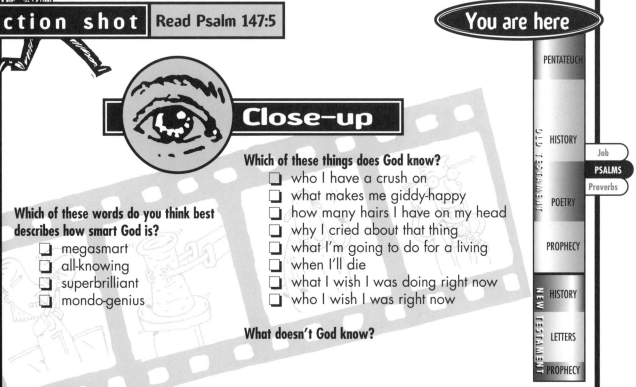

Close-up

Which of these words do you think best describes how smart God is?
- ☐ megasmart
- ☐ all-knowing
- ☐ superbrilliant
- ☐ mondo-genius

Which of these things does God know?
- ☐ who I have a crush on
- ☐ what makes me giddy-happy
- ☐ how many hairs I have on my head
- ☐ why I cried about that thing
- ☐ what I'm going to do for a living
- ☐ when I'll die
- ☐ what I wish I was doing right now
- ☐ who I wish I was right now

What doesn't God know?

You are here

PENTATEUCH

OLD TESTAMENT

HISTORY — Job

PSALMS

POETRY — Proverbs

PROPHECY

NEW TESTAMENT

HISTORY

LETTERS

PROPHECY

What difference does it make that God's so smart?

Self-portrait

While you're filling out this page, don't think about whether or not you're a good student. Don't think about whether or not you get good grades or who thinks you're smart or not. We're going to talk about a different kind of smart. We're going to talk about how much you know God.

How God-smart are you? Add a needle to this meter to show your answer.

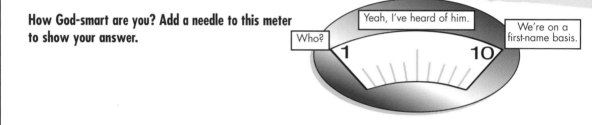

Who?

Yeah, I've heard of him.

We're on a first-name basis.

1   10

Think hard about this one: Where have you seen God at work in your life?

If you want to learn more about God, it's important to find him in action. Rate each of these from 1 to 10 to show whether you think this is a good place to see God in action.

(1 = not gonna find God there!; 10 = awesome place to see God in action)

___ in little children   ___ in nature   ___ in other Christians

___ in the Bible   ___ in my life   ___ in my youth group

___ in Christian music   ___ in history   ___ in surprising places

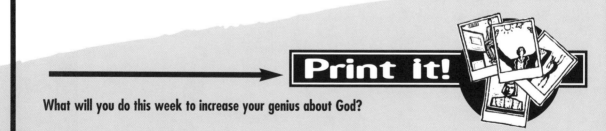

Print it!

What will you do this week to increase your genius about God?

God is like a
DREAMER

Delight yourself in the Lord and he will give you the desires of your heart. Commit your way to the Lord; trust in him and he will do this. Psalm 37:4-5

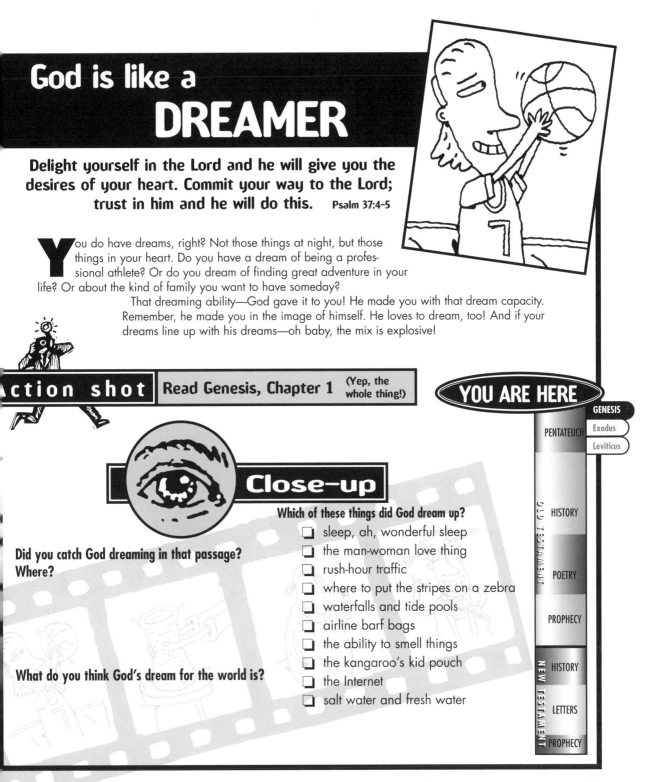

You do have dreams, right? Not those things at night, but those things in your heart. Do you have a dream of being a professional athlete? Or do you dream of finding great adventure in your life? Or about the kind of family you want to have someday?

That dreaming ability—God gave it to you! He made you with that dream capacity. Remember, he made you in the image of himself. He loves to dream, too! And if your dreams line up with his dreams—oh baby, the mix is explosive!

action shot Read Genesis, Chapter 1 (Yep, the whole thing!)

YOU ARE HERE

Close-up

Did you catch God dreaming in that passage? Where?

What do you think God's dream for the world is?

Which of these things did God dream up?

- ☐ sleep, ah, wonderful sleep
- ☐ the man-woman love thing
- ☐ rush-hour traffic
- ☐ where to put the stripes on a zebra
- ☐ waterfalls and tide pools
- ☐ airline barf bags
- ☐ the ability to smell things
- ☐ the kangaroo's kid pouch
- ☐ the Internet
- ☐ salt water and fresh water

GENESIS
PENTATEUCH | Exodus
Leviticus

OLD TESTAMENT
HISTORY

POETRY

PROPHECY

NEW TESTAMENT
HISTORY

LETTERS

PROPHECY

What are some of the coolest things that people (made in God's image) have dreamed up?

How about a life dream? What's something you dream about being or doing?

When is dreaming good? When is dreaming not so good?

Print it!

Write a prayer or note to God telling him one of the dreams of your heart.

God is like a
VOiCE

The voice of the Lord is powerful; the voice of the Lord is majestic. Psalm 29:4

Ever heard God's voice? An out-loud voice? Most people haven't. Even in Bible times, when it seems like God was talking out loud to people all the time, he still saved his sky-talk for special occasions—the birth of his nation, dictating the Ten Commandments, his Son's baptism, events like that. It wasn't every day that people heard the Voice.

But he still speaks to people every day. You don't usually hear his voice in the same way you hear music or a friend talking. Sometimes you hear God in your head or your heart.

action shot | Read Revelation 3:20

Close-up

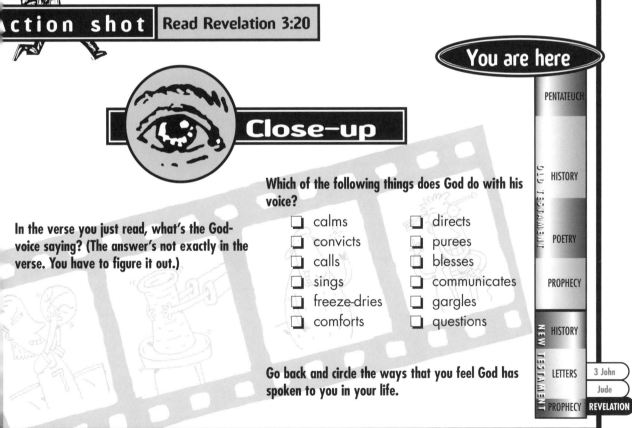

In the verse you just read, what's the God-voice saying? (The answer's not exactly in the verse. You have to figure it out.)

Which of the following things does God do with his voice?

- ☐ calms
- ☐ convicts
- ☐ calls
- ☐ sings
- ☐ freeze-dries
- ☐ comforts
- ☑ directs
- ☑ purees
- ☐ blesses
- ☐ communicates
- ☐ gargles
- ☐ questions

Go back and circle the ways that you feel God has spoken to you in your life.

You are here

PENTATEUCH

HISTORY — OLD TESTAMENT

POETRY

PROPHECY

HISTORY — NEW TESTAMENT

LETTERS — 3 John / Jude

PROPHECY — REVELATION

How does God usually speak to you?

Self-portrait

Which of the following things do you do with your voice? (Be honest!)

❏ scream	❏ joke	❏ sing	❏ praise
❏ calm	❏ direct	❏ convict	❏ swear
❏ call	❏ bless	❏ communicate	❏ yell
❏ pray	❏ comfort	❏ question	❏ encourage
❏ complain	❏ laugh	❏ tease	

Customize the list you just finished in these ways—
1. Underline the things you can do with your voice that would please God.
2. Put x's next to the things that would *not* please God.
3. Circle the things you do every single day.
4. Put an exclamation point next to the four things you do most often with your voice.

How can your voice be like God's? Got an example?

Print it!

Go back to the first Self-Portrait question. Put stars before and after the *one thing* you're going to try to do more of this week.

God is like a
LiGHT

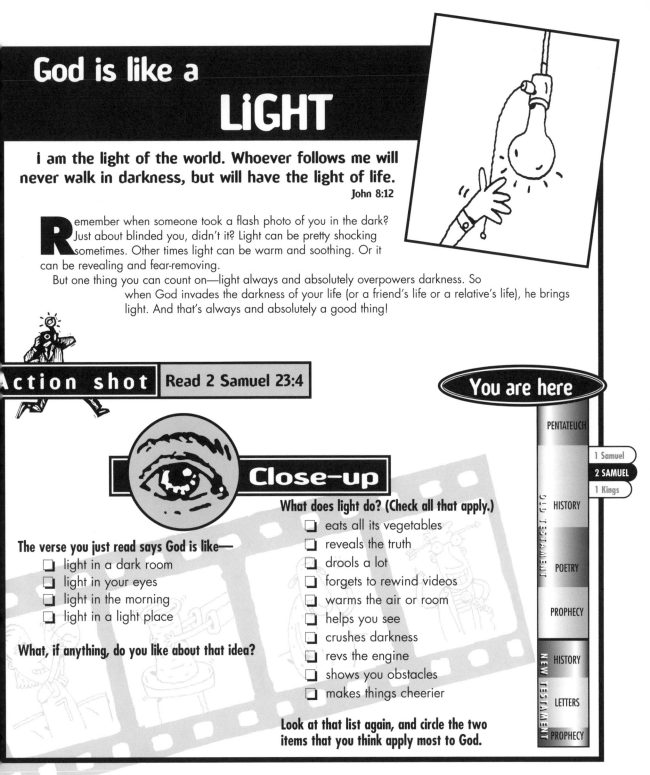

i am the light of the world. Whoever follows me will never walk in darkness, but will have the light of life.
John 8:12

Remember when someone took a flash photo of you in the dark? Just about blinded you, didn't it? Light can be pretty shocking sometimes. Other times light can be warm and soothing. Or it can be revealing and fear-removing.

But one thing you can count on—light always and absolutely overpowers darkness. So when God invades the darkness of your life (or a friend's life or a relative's life), he brings light. And that's always and absolutely a good thing!

Action shot | Read 2 Samuel 23:4

Close-up

The verse you just read says God is like—
- ❑ light in a dark room
- ❑ light in your eyes
- ❑ light in the morning
- ❑ light in a light place

What, if anything, do you like about that idea?

What does light do? (Check all that apply.)
- ❑ eats all its vegetables
- ❑ reveals the truth
- ❑ drools a lot
- ❑ forgets to rewind videos
- ❑ warms the air or room
- ❑ helps you see
- ❑ crushes darkness
- ❑ revs the engine
- ❑ shows you obstacles
- ❑ makes things cheerier

Look at that list again, and circle the two items that you think apply most to God.

You are here

PENTATEUCH

1 Samuel
2 SAMUEL
1 Kings

OLD TESTAMENT
HISTORY

POETRY

PROPHECY

NEW TESTAMENT
HISTORY

LETTERS

PROPHECY

Rate the light-ness of these students.

- Ronda and her friends are at a party, and there are a bunch of kids drinking beer. Ronda's friends are thinking about helping themselves to some, too. Ronda tells them she won't and doesn't think they should either.

How is or how isn't Ronda like light in this story?

Rate Ronda's light-ness. Add a needle to this meter to show your answer.

- Sara's dad has been having a fight with his brother (Sara's uncle) for, like, five thousand years. And it's over something really small and stupid. Sara kindly suggests to her dad that he should think about forgiving his brother and work at repairing the relationship.

How is or how isn't Sara like light in this story?

Rate Sara's light-ness. Add a needle to this meter to show your answer.

How about you? How's your light-ness in these areas? *Add needles to these 4 meters to show your answers.*

Do you help people see the way to go and help them make good choices?	Are you warm to people, like the morning sun?	Do you help people see obstacles in their lives?	Are you honest and truthful?

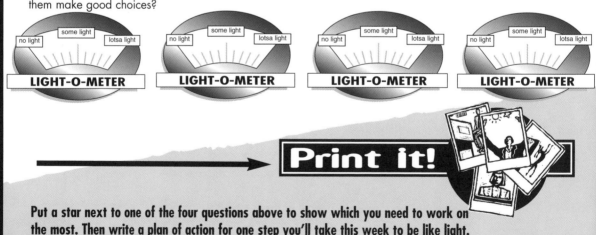

Put a star next to one of the four questions above to show which you need to work on the most. Then write a plan of action for one step you'll take this week to be like light.

God is like an ARTIST

The heavens declare the glory of God; the skies proclaim the work of his hands. Psalm 19:1

Some art you like, some art you hate. Even great art is *simply amazing* to some people and *whatever* to others. But there's one artist that blows everyone's mind with his creativity. In fact, every single painter, sculptor, and photographer has copied this artist's work since he first set down his pallet of paints. That artist is God. (you, being smarter than the average junior higher had already guessed that, since this is a book about God!)

Orange and pink and red sunsets. Black and white zebras. Blue shadows. Black, brown, reddish-brown, pinkish, and many other colors of people. Deep green emeralds and leaves and frogs. Rainbow-colored, well, rainbows. God made them all. He even came up with the colors! And think of it: you're his best piece of art ever.

Action shot | Read Psalm 111:2–4

You are here

Close-up

What's one of God's art creations you find totally spectacular?

What do you like about how God painted you?

PENTATEUCH

OLD TESTAMENT

HISTORY

Job

PSALMS

Proverbs

POETRY

PROPHECY

NEW TESTAMENT

HISTORY

LETTERS

PROPHECY

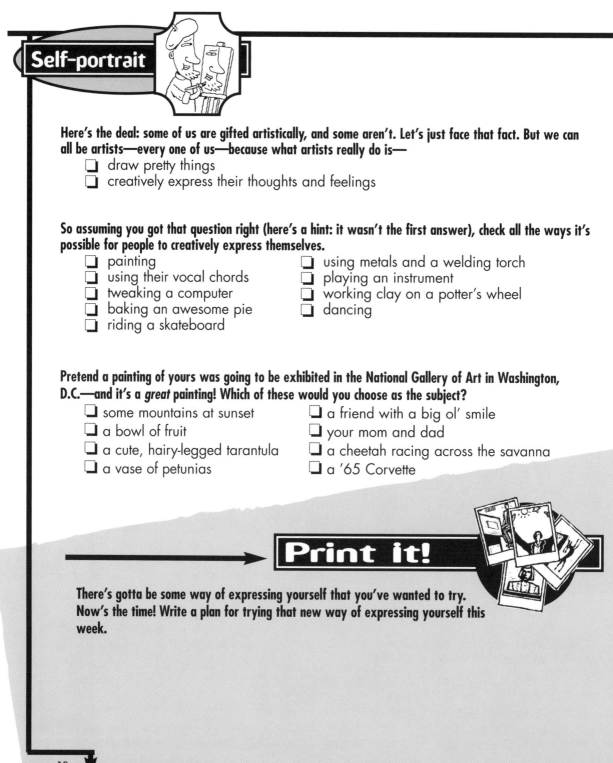

Self-portrait

Here's the deal: some of us are gifted artistically, and some aren't. Let's just face that fact. But we can all be artists—every one of us—because what artists really do is—

❏ draw pretty things
❏ creatively express their thoughts and feelings

So assuming you got that question right (here's a hint: it wasn't the first answer), check all the ways it's possible for people to creatively express themselves.

❏ painting
❏ using their vocal chords
❏ tweaking a computer
❏ baking an awesome pie
❏ riding a skateboard
❏ using metals and a welding torch
❏ playing an instrument
❏ working clay on a potter's wheel
❏ dancing

Pretend a painting of yours was going to be exhibited in the National Gallery of Art in Washington, D.C.—and it's a *great* painting! Which of these would you choose as the subject?

❏ some mountains at sunset
❏ a bowl of fruit
❏ a cute, hairy-legged tarantula
❏ a vase of petunias
❏ a friend with a big ol' smile
❏ your mom and dad
❏ a cheetah racing across the savanna
❏ a '65 Corvette

Print it!

There's gotta be some way of expressing yourself that you've wanted to try. Now's the time! Write a plan for trying that new way of expressing yourself this week.

God is like a
DOCTOR

He heals the brokenhearted and binds up their wounds.
Psalm 147:3

If you've ever been big-time hurt or sick, you know how important a doctor is. Here's this person who knows much more about your body than you do—she can figure things out and help get you fixed up and back to your normal self.

Doctors may know lots more than you, but they still know only *some* things about your body. On the other hand, God—the supa-dupa doctor—*made* you! So don't you think he knows more about your body than any doctor does? It gets better. God can heal more than physical problems. He can heal your heart. And there's no better mending to be done!

Action shot | Read Psalm 30:2

You are here

Close-up

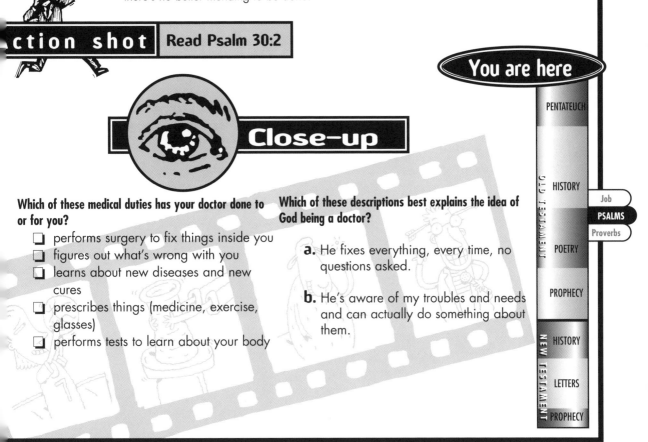

Which of these medical duties has your doctor done to or for you?

❑ performs surgery to fix things inside you
❑ figures out what's wrong with you
❑ learns about new diseases and new cures
❑ prescribes things (medicine, exercise, glasses)
❑ performs tests to learn about your body

Which of these descriptions best explains the idea of God being a doctor?

a. He fixes everything, every time, no questions asked.

b. He's aware of my troubles and needs and can actually do something about them.

PENTATEUCH

OLD TESTAMENT

HISTORY | Job

PSALMS

Proverbs

POETRY

PROPHECY

NEW TESTAMENT

HISTORY

LETTERS

PROPHECY

So how are *you* at exercising your made-in-the-image-of-God doctoring abilities? Color in this blood-pressure meter to rate how well you deal with Cindy's and Max's situations below.

I notice every single need in the entire world and help each of those people. ➡

I sometimes notice needs and occasionally try to help meet them. ➡

I've never, ever noticed or helped a single person's need in my whole life. ➡

Cindy complains about being tired all the time. You know her mom works two jobs, and Cindy has to do tons of the work around the house. What needs might Cindy have, and what could you do to help her?

Max sits by himself at lunch every day. There's nothing really wrong with him, other than he's in a wheelchair. You've never seen him smile. What needs do you think Max has? What could you do to help him?

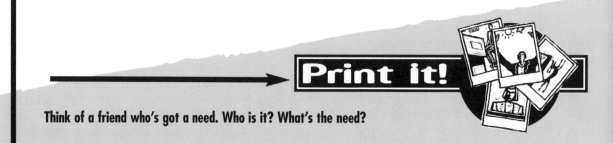

Print it!

Think of a friend who's got a need. Who is it? What's the need?

What can you, Doctor _____ (put your name there), do to help meet that need this week?

God is like a
SWORDSMAN

Take the helmet of salvation and the sword of the Spirit, which is the word of God. Ephesians 6:17

We like to think of God as a cuddly daddy (which he is). But just when you think you've got a picture that sums up exactly who God is, he surprises you with yet *another* aspect of his greatness.

And this sword thing is one of them. God is pure and can't tolerate evil. So evil is gonna take a lickin'. God's sword is going to slice and dice, and it won't be pretty. Something else about God the Swordsman—he cuts through the baloney to get to the truth. And he always gets deep down into the truth because he *is* truth.

Action shot | Read Hebrews 4:12

Close-up

What does this verse say God's sword does?

Do you have any attitudes of the heart that need to be cut out? What are they?
(Big hint: these could be things like rebellion, disobedience, disrespect, anger, jealousy, greed, and so on.)

pokes

penetrates

makes a cool chinking sound when it hits things

thrusts

divides soul and spirit

judges thoughts

You are here

PENTATEUCH

OLD TESTAMENT

HISTORY

POETRY

PROPHECY

NEW TESTAMENT

HISTORY

LETTERS

PROPHECY

Philemon

HEBREWS

James

God's sword gets to the truth. Below is a bunch of statements that you would *think* are true if you believe commercials and the kids at your school. Stab through each one with the sword of truth, and write the real deal below it.

- Everybody's having sex. And if you don't, something's wrong with you.

- Parents are idiots. You know much more than they do.

- Drinking and partying are part of life. Every teenager on the face of the earth does them.

- Life sucks unless you're rich.

- Just because something's wrong for me doesn't make it wrong for you.

Good job! You've passed Junior Swordsman Training! Now—what's another pile of baloney you're faced with that you can wield the sword on?

Point (carefully!) the sword at yourself for a minute. What's an area of your life where you haven't been totally honest—either with yourself or with someone else?

Print it!

What are a couple of ways you can learn to be a better swordsman?

God is like LiFE

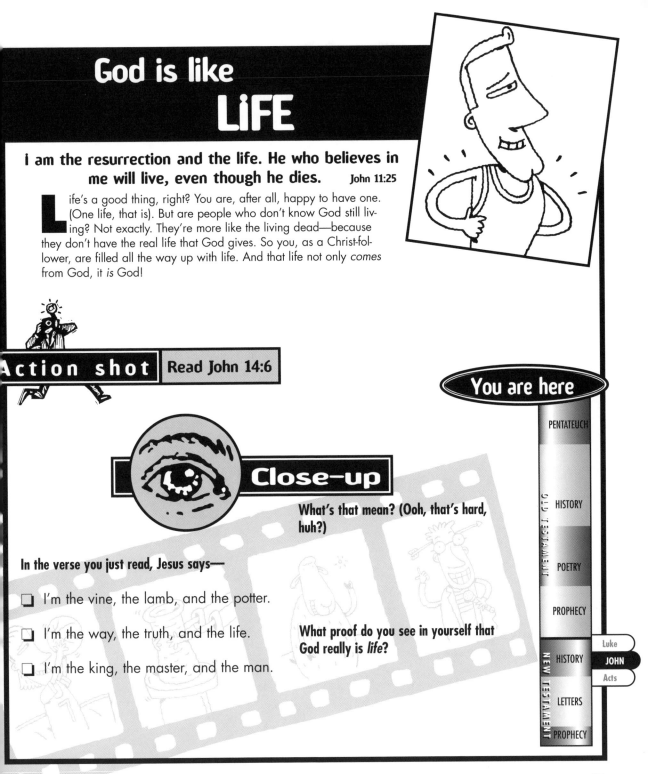

i am the resurrection and the life. He who believes in me will live, even though he dies. John 11:25

Life's a good thing, right? You are, after all, happy to have one. (One life, that is). But are people who don't know God still living? Not exactly. They're more like the living dead—because they don't have the real life that God gives. So you, as a Christ-follower, are filled all the way up with life. And that life not only *comes* from God, it *is* God!

Action shot | Read John 14:6

Close-up

What's that mean? (Ooh, that's hard, huh?)

In the verse you just read, Jesus says—

❏ I'm the vine, the lamb, and the potter.

❏ I'm the way, the truth, and the life.

❏ I'm the king, the master, and the man.

What proof do you see in yourself that God really is *life*?

You are here

PENTATEUCH

OLD TESTAMENT

HISTORY

POETRY

PROPHECY

NEW TESTAMENT

HISTORY

Luke
JOHN
Acts

LETTERS

PROPHECY

Self-portrait

Can you snap your fingers and make life begin? Can you create life from nothing? Okay, then you're probably not God. But you can still be a life-giving person!

Meet Dave and Kate. Which of these junior highers is most life-giving? Circle the story.

Dave's dad has been totally stressed lately, working late and on weekends. Tonight, when Dave's dad got home, Dave had the lawn mowed and the trash cans taken out so his dad wouldn't have to ask him to do those chores.

Grace hates the way she laughs—kinda loud and goofy. She's tried to change it but always forgets until it's too late. But today Kate looked her right in the eyes and said, "I love the way you laugh, Grace. It makes me happy."

Write two life-giving things you could do.

1.

2.

Choose one of these to describe yourself.

❑ I'm a big-time life-giver—always looking for ways to make people feel encouraged.

❑ I'm learning to be a life-giver. I try to do that stuff but usually forget.

❑ I have no idea what this life-giver stuff is all about. I guess I'll talk to my youth leader.

Right now (like in the next five minutes), go say something life-giving to someone. Go. C'mon, stop reading this and do it. We're serious. Really.

God is like a ROOMMATE

> i pray that out of his glorious riches he may strengthen you with power through his Spirit in your inner being, so that Christ may dwell in your hearts through faith. **Ephesians 3:16-17**

When you ask Jesus into your life, he says yes! But he doesn't just say it—he moves in! Jesus becomes your roommate. He brings with him all his stuff—purity, comfort, love, hope. But he's kind of a picky roommate. It really, really bugs him when you leave the house messy (we're not talking about your bedroom here—we're talking about your *life*).

He's a great roommate. But he kinda likes things done his way. Of course, his way sure is best.

Action shot | Read Colossians 1:27

Close-up

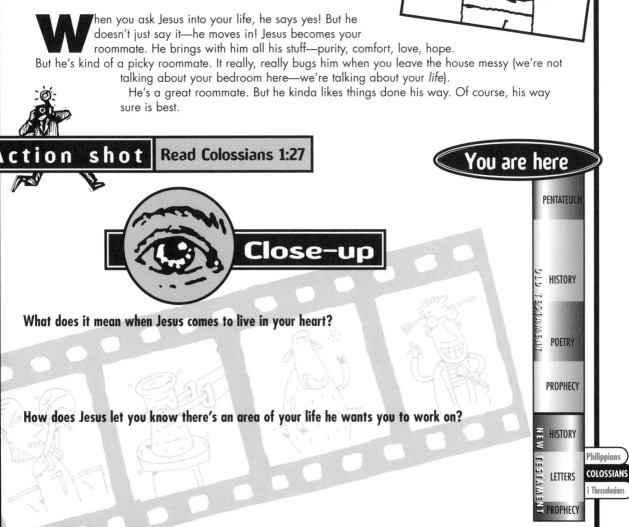

What does it mean when Jesus comes to live in your heart?

How does Jesus let you know there's an area of your life he wants you to work on?

You are here

OLD TESTAMENT
- PENTATEUCH
- HISTORY
- POETRY
- PROPHECY

NEW TESTAMENT
- HISTORY
- LETTERS
- PROPHECY

Philippians
COLOSSIANS
1 Thessalonians

Self-portrait

What parts of your life have you let Jesus move into? What parts have you kept him out of? (Think hard on this one.)

For each of the following, circle the areas you let Jesus into, cross out the areas where you haven't let him into at all, and draw a wavy line under the ones you've let him into a little bit.

my friendships	my family relationships
my schoolwork	my play time and hobbies
my enemies	my choices about TV, movies, and music
my faith and spiritual life	my church friends and church involvement
my social life	my thinking about the future (job, life)

What's an area of your life you think he might want to work on? (If you have a hard time answering this, look at your answers to the first question on this page.)

What can you do to start working on this area with him?

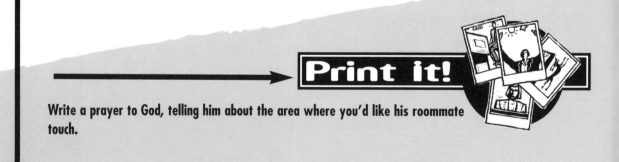

Print it!

Write a prayer to God, telling him about the area where you'd like his roommate touch.

God is like a
GiFT

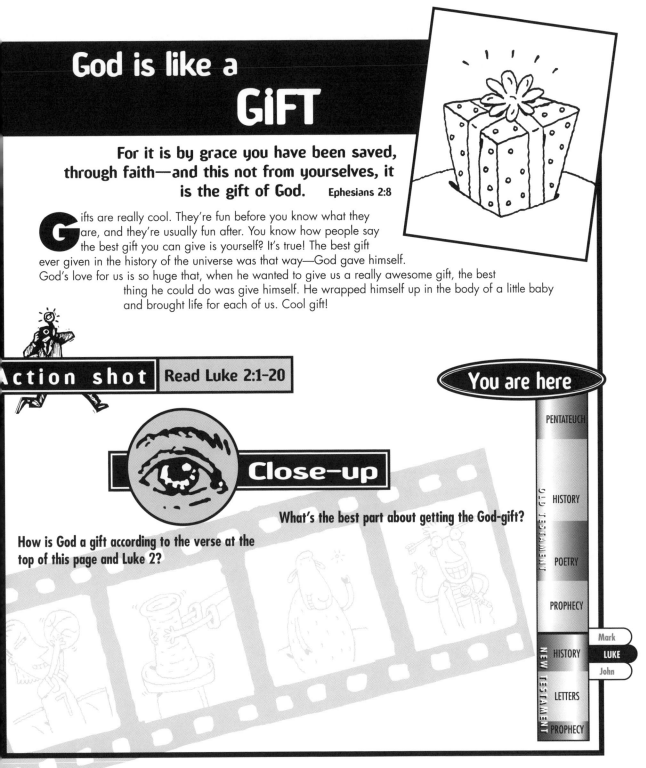

For it is by grace you have been saved, through faith—and this not from yourselves, it is the gift of God. Ephesians 2:8

Gifts are really cool. They're fun before you know what they are, and they're usually fun after. You know how people say the best gift you can give is yourself? It's true! The best gift ever given in the history of the universe was that way—God gave himself.

God's love for us is so huge that, when he wanted to give us a really awesome gift, the best thing he could do was give himself. He wrapped himself up in the body of a little baby and brought life for each of us. Cool gift!

Action shot Read Luke 2:1-20

Close-up

What's the best part about getting the God-gift?

How is God a gift according to the verse at the top of this page and Luke 2?

You are here

PENTATEUCH

OLD TESTAMENT

HISTORY

POETRY

PROPHECY

NEW TESTAMENT

HISTORY

Mark
LUKE
John

LETTERS

PROPHECY

Self-portrait

What's the best gift you ever received? What's the best gift you ever gave?

You can be a gift to other people. Order the following ideas from 1 ("I could definitely be a gift in this way") to 8 ("No way I could ever be a gift in this way").

___ Write an encouraging letter to someone who's not your best friend.

___ Sit with a lonely kid at lunch.

___ Do one of your brother's or sister's chores without expecting anything in return.

___ Tell your mom and dad you love them.

___ Make cookies for a family friend.

___ Visit an elderly neighbor.

___ Thank your pastor for all his hard work.

___ Volunteer for a day at a local charity or community center.

Now look back over the list and choose one that you'll try this week. Circle it. Or write another plan here.

One more question. How can you be a gift to God this week?

God is like a
HEN

> How often I have longed to gather your children together,
> as a hen gathers her chicks under her wings,
> but you were not willing! **Luke 13:34**

Wait a minute—God is like a *hen*? But isn't a hen a female chicken? Yes. And isn't chicken the main ingredient in McNuggets? Yes again. But we're talking about chicken, not McNuggets. So here's probably the only way a hen reminds you a whole lot of God: the moment you threaten a hen's chicks, this almost-flightless bird with the bobbing head and silly walk is transformed into a storm of wings and feathers, pecking beak, scratching claws, and ear-shattering squawking. If she succeeds in stopping your invasion, she gathers her chicks about her and spreads her wings over them in protection. If you want to get at one of her chicks, you'll have to go through her to get it. And that's a really good picture of God.

Action shot   Read Psalm 91:4

Close-up

You are here

What's the safest, most cuddly place you can think of? Why does that place seem safe to you?

If you were a little chick, why would it feel safe under your mom's wings? (Check all that apply.)

- ❑ no mean ol' foxes under there
- ❑ it's got that mom-smell
- ❑ it's soft and warm
- ❑ great security alarm system!

PENTATEUCH

OLD TESTAMENT

HISTORY

Job
PSALMS
Proverbs

POETRY

PROPHECY

NEW TESTAMENT

HISTORY

LETTERS

PROPHECY

What difference does it make that God wants to be a mother hen to you? (Check all that apply.)

- ❏ It makes me feel safe and protected.
- ❏ It doesn't make any difference.
- ❏ It makes me thankful.
- ❏ I don't get it.

Self-portrait

Last week, all the kids at school started spreading mean and untrue rumors about Kirsten's friend Lara and some guy from another school. Lara doesn't even know the guy or how or why the rumors started. Kirsten just read about God being like a hen and thought that maybe there was some way she should be like a hen to Lara. But Kirsten knows that the rest of the kids at school will be major jerks to her if she defends Lara. And she doesn't want to treat Lara like a little kid. What should Kirsten do? How can she put this hen example into practice in a way that makes Lara feel safe and protected?

What are some ways that junior highers can make people feel safe and protected?

Print it!

Think of someone who could use a little protection and safety. What can you do about it, specifically?

God is like RAIN

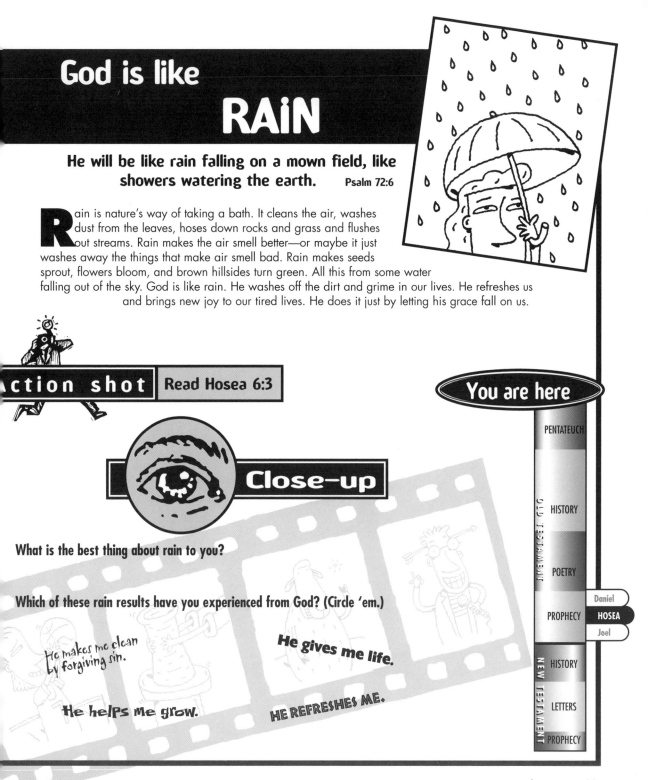

He will be like rain falling on a mown field, like showers watering the earth. Psalm 72:6

Rain is nature's way of taking a bath. It cleans the air, washes dust from the leaves, hoses down rocks and grass and flushes out streams. Rain makes the air smell better—or maybe it just washes away the things that make air smell bad. Rain makes seeds sprout, flowers bloom, and brown hillsides turn green. All this from some water falling out of the sky. God is like rain. He washes off the dirt and grime in our lives. He refreshes us and brings new joy to our tired lives. He does it just by letting his grace fall on us.

Action shot   Read Hosea 6:3

Close-up

What is the best thing about rain to you?

Which of these rain results have you experienced from God? (Circle 'em.)

He makes me clean by forgiving sin.

He gives me life.

He helps me grow.

HE REFRESHES ME.

You are here

PENTATEUCH

OLD TESTAMENT

HISTORY

POETRY

PROPHECY

Daniel
HOSEA
Joel

NEW TESTAMENT

HISTORY

LETTERS

PROPHECY

Give yourself a rain rating. Circle the amount of rain you think represents your commitment to each of the following actions.

I try to refresh people with my words. I offer compliments and am quick to thank people for things they do. I encourage people whenever I can.

I'm a forgiving person. I know it's really God who forgives, but I can model God's forgiveness by how I treat people. Even if they're jerks to me, I try to forgive them.

I encourage growth in people's lives. I am growing myself, too! I help my friends and family see areas where they could grow; then I encourage them in those directions.

I'm a life-giver. I don't really give life like God does, but I try to be positive with people and bring freshness to relationships, conversations, and situations.

Print it!

Put a big honkin' star next to one of the four statements above to represent one you'll work on this week. Then write a plan for how you'll do this.

God is like a
PARTY HOST

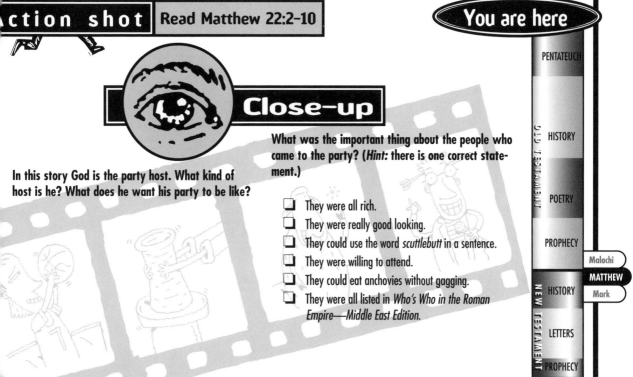

i have come that they may have life, and have it to the full. John 10:10

Some parties are really exclusive—you have to be important to be invited. And that was even more true back when the Bible was written. So God, the ultimate party host (hangin' out for a while as Jesus), tells a story to blow away this idea.

"All you fancy-schmancy people, you're so busy worrying about all your stuff and your importance that you're missing my party," Jesus says in so many words. "But the regular people, the imperfect people, the lonely people, the hurting people, those who some think are unacceptable—*those* are the people I want at my party. And it's going to be a party like no other party, ever, in the history or future of the world!"

So are you regular? Are you imperfect? Are you lonely or hurting or unacceptable? God accepts you! More than that, he wants to host you at the two ultimate parties of the universe—life with him here on earth and life forever in heaven.

Action shot — Read Matthew 22:2–10

Close-up

In this story God is the party host. What kind of host is he? What does he want his party to be like?

What was the important thing about the people who came to the party? (*Hint:* there is one correct statement.)

- ☐ They were all rich.
- ☐ They were really good looking.
- ☐ They could use the word *scuttlebutt* in a sentence.
- ☐ They were willing to attend.
- ☐ They could eat anchovies without gagging.
- ☐ They were all listed in *Who's Who in the Roman Empire—Middle East Edition*.

You are here

OLD TESTAMENT
- PENTATEUCH
- HISTORY
- POETRY
- PROPHECY

NEW TESTAMENT
- HISTORY
- LETTERS
- PROPHECY

Malachi
MATTHEW
Mark

The verse at the top of the previous page says God wants you to have life to the full. God's party isn't just in heaven. He wants you to have a great life *now!* What do you think life "to the full" means?

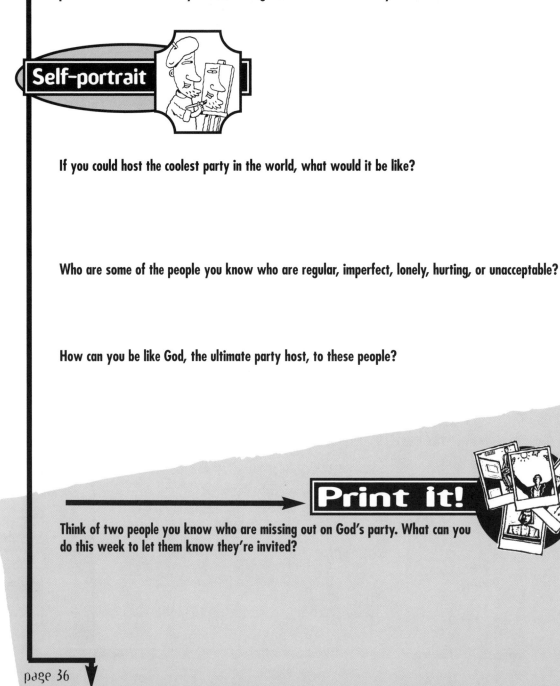

Self-portrait

If you could host the coolest party in the world, what would it be like?

Who are some of the people you know who are regular, imperfect, lonely, hurting, or unacceptable?

How can you be like God, the ultimate party host, to these people?

Print it!

Think of two people you know who are missing out on God's party. What can you do this week to let them know they're invited?

God is like a
BOSS

Well done, good and faithful servant! You have been faithful with a few things; I will put you in charge of many things. Come and share your master's happiness! Matthew 25:21

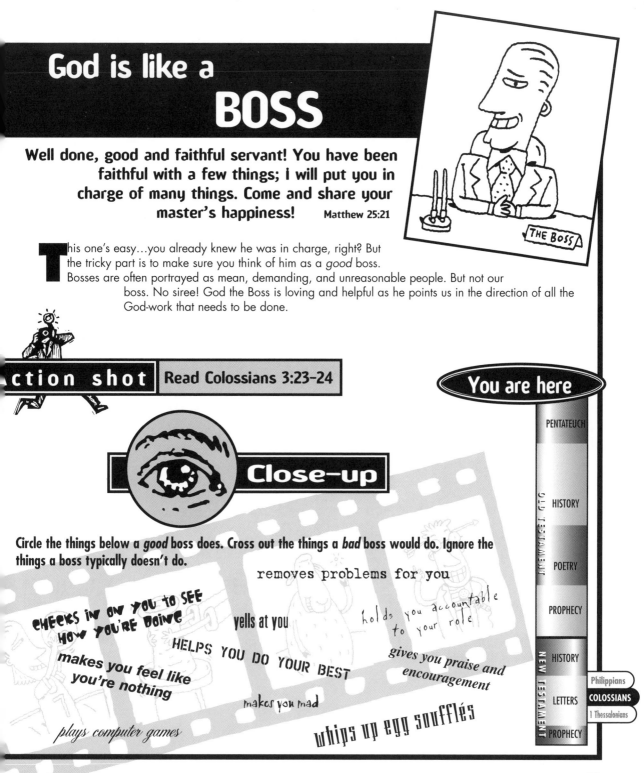

THE BOSS

This one's easy...you already knew he was in charge, right? But the tricky part is to make sure you think of him as a *good* boss. Bosses are often portrayed as mean, demanding, and unreasonable people. But not our boss. No siree! God the Boss is loving and helpful as he points us in the direction of all the God-work that needs to be done.

ction shot Read Colossians 3:23-24

Close-up

Circle the things below a *good* boss does. Cross out the things a *bad* boss would do. Ignore the things a boss typically doesn't do.

removes problems for you

CHECKS IN ON YOU TO SEE HOW YOU'RE DOING

yells at you

holds you accountable to your role

HELPS YOU DO YOUR BEST

makes you feel like you're nothing

gives you praise and encouragement

makes you mad

plays computer games

whips up egg soufflés

You are here

PENTATEUCH

OLD TESTAMENT

HISTORY

POETRY

PROPHECY

NEW TESTAMENT

HISTORY

Philippians

COLOSSIANS

LETTERS

1 Thessalonians

PROPHECY

Self-portrait

What kinds of things does God the Boss want you to be doing?

That Matthew 25 verse at the top of the previous page is from a story Jesus tells about a boss who puts his servants in charge of his possessions. What things have you been put in charge of?

How well do you manage these things?
- ❑ I don't take care of the things I've been put in charge of. I deserve a closet for an office.
- ❑ I'm pretty sloppy with my things and don't pay attention to them. I've earned a cubicle for my office.
- ❑ I'm responsible with the things I'm in charge of, but sometimes I forget or get lazy. I should get a regular office.
- ❑ I'm very responsible with the things I've been put in charge of. I've earned a big corner office with a view.

Finish this sentence: *I'm the kind of boss who—*

Being a boss over the things in my life really means—

- ❑ being bossy
- ❑ being responsible
- ❑ being important
- ❑ being pushy and demanding

Print it!

What's one responsibility in your life where you've been a sloppy boss?
What can you do about it this week?

God is like a ROCK

From the ends of the earth i call to you, i call as my heart grows faint; lead me to the rock that is higher than i. Psalm 61:2

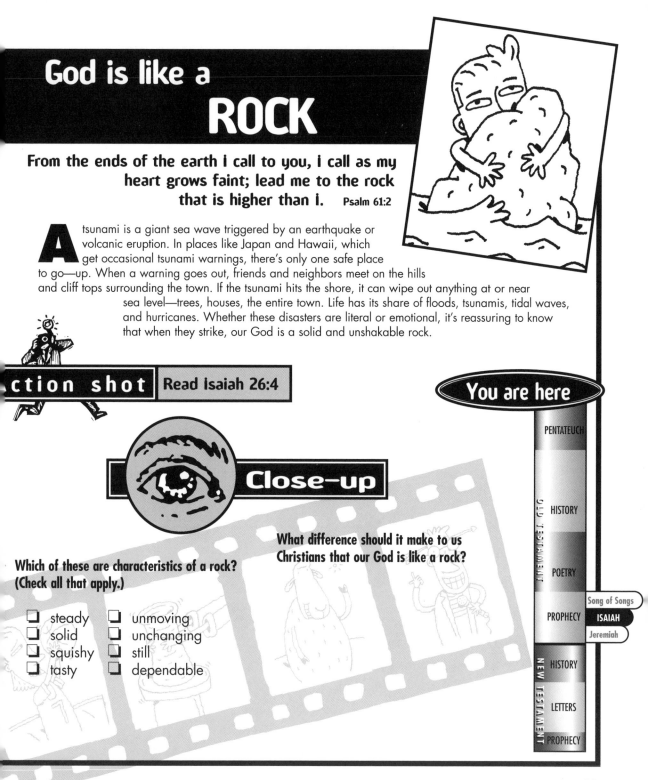

A tsunami is a giant sea wave triggered by an earthquake or volcanic eruption. In places like Japan and Hawaii, which get occasional tsunami warnings, there's only one safe place to go—up. When a warning goes out, friends and neighbors meet on the hills and cliff tops surrounding the town. If the tsunami hits the shore, it can wipe out anything at or near sea level—trees, houses, the entire town. Life has its share of floods, tsunamis, tidal waves, and hurricanes. Whether these disasters are literal or emotional, it's reassuring to know that when they strike, our God is a solid and unshakable rock.

ction shot   Read isaiah 26:4

Close-up

You are here

Which of these are characteristics of a rock? (Check all that apply.)

- ☐ steady
- ☐ solid
- ☑ squishy
- ☐ tasty
- ☐ unmoving
- ☐ unchanging
- ☐ still
- ☐ dependable

What difference should it make to us Christians that our God is like a rock?

PENTATEUCH

HISTORY

OLD TESTAMENT

POETRY

Song of Songs

PROPHECY   ISAIAH

Jeremiah

HISTORY

NEW TESTAMENT

LETTERS

PROPHECY

Of the rock-like characteristics from the list on the previous page, which ones would people use to describe you? (Check all that apply.)

❏ steady ❏ unmoving ❏ solid
❏ unchanging ❏ still ❏ dependable

Answer one of these two questions.

If you checked at least one of those boxes, answer this question: Why would people describe you with the words you checked?

If you checked none of the boxes, answer this question: Why wouldn't people use any of those words to describe you?

If a friend is going through a tough time, how much can he count on you to be there?

I'm like dough.
A friend can't count on me at all.

I'm like superball rubber.
A friend can count on me sometimes, but not all the time.

I'm a rock.
A friend can count on me always, without fail.

If your life were secretly videotaped and then shown to you, would you see yourself acting the same around everyone? Or do you constantly change who you are according to who you're with?

I'm a shape-shifter.
I'm a totally different person at church than I am at school.

I'm a semi-mutant.
I only change a little bit.

I'm a rock.
I am who I am, no changing.

Print it!

Which rock characteristic do you think you'd like to work on in your life?
What can you do about it?

God is like a LAMB

The next day John saw Jesus coming toward him and said, "Look, the Lamb of God, who takes away the sin of the world!" John 1:29

One of the most costly sacrifices God told the Jews to make was killing a year-old lamb—with *no* defects—to pay for their sins. This meant that just when these perfect yearlings were getting old enough to earn their keep by providing wool or young 'uns—they were given to God. It was a *real* sacrifice. This reminded them that their sin was costly—their sin hurt God deeply and stood in the way of making Israel a great and powerful nation. Today you're going to figure out why God is like one of these lambs.

Action shot | Read Revelation 5:12

Close-up

What was the result of sacrificing a lamb?
- [ ] a dead lamb
- [ ] lamb meat
- [ ] forgiven sins
- [ ] all of these

Why is Jesus called the Lamb of God?
- [ ] because he was the ultimate sacrifice for our sins
- [ ] because he's, like, God's pet
- [ ] because he…um…actually, I don't have a clue

Assuming you checked the first box in the previous question (which is the correct answer, by the way), why was God willing to make such a huge sacrifice for you?

You are here

OLD TESTAMENT	
PENTATEUCH	
HISTORY	
POETRY	
PROPHECY	

NEW TESTAMENT	
HISTORY	
LETTERS	3 John
	Jude
PROPHECY	REVELATION

Self-portrait

Yes, you too can be a lamb! Well, not exactly the sort that takes away people's sins...but you can still _____ with your life.

Choose one of these options to fill in the blank

- ❏ make a mess
- ❏ make instant pudding
- ❏ make sacrifices
- ❏ make good things

Who below made the biggest sacrifice, Garrett or Teresa? Circle one of 'em.

Garrett had saved up almost enough money to buy a new CD when he heard about a kid at church who couldn't afford to go to summer camp. Garrett gave his money to help the other kid go to camp.

Teresa was looking forward to going to her friend Jan's. When the baby sitter for Teresa's baby brother canceled, her mom was going to have to stay home from her date. Teresa canceled her plans with Jan and baby-sat her brother so her mom could go on her date.

If you suspected there was no right answer to this question, you're right—both kids made big sacrifices. What other ways can teenagers like you make sacrifices? (Try to think of at least four more.)

Print it!

What's one sacrifice you can make this week that will honor God?

God is like a COUNSELOR

All this also comes from the Lord Almighty, wonderful in counsel and magnificent in wisdom. Isaiah 28:29

There are all kinds of counselors—marriage and family counselors, legal counselors, spiritual counselors, camp counselors, career counselors, guidance counselors. Whatever kind of counselors they are, they should *all* be wise at giving advice and direction. Still, some counselors aren't as good at this as others. There's *one* counselor who sets the mark that all other counselors are measured by. Can you guess who?

Action shot | Read Psalm 32:8

Close-up

Which of these best describes a good counselor?

❏ Someone who takes your money while you sit there and talk.

❏ Anyone who listens to you and makes a suggestion about what you might do.

How is God like a counselor?

Pretend this door is the door to Jesus' counseling office. What words do you think would be on the door? (Go ahead and write them on the door as you think they'd look.)

You are here

PENTATEUCH

OLD TESTAMENT

HISTORY

Job
PSALMS
Proverbs

POETRY

PROPHECY

NEW TESTAMENT

HISTORY

LETTERS

PROPHECY

Circle *agree* or *disagree* for each of these statements.

agree   disagree   I would have to go to a special school to be a counselor.

agree   disagree   I would have to have an important-looking degree with letters
                       after my name to be a counselor.

agree   disagree   Only adults can be counselors.

agree   disagree   The most important part of being a counselor is giving advice.

You know what? *All* those statements are disagree-able.

How can middle schoolers be counselors?

If the most important part of being a counselor isn't giving advice, then what is it? (*Hint:* It involves a matched set of things.)

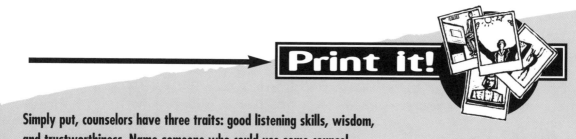

Print it!

Simply put, counselors have three traits: good listening skills, wisdom,
and trustworthiness. Name someone who could use some counsel
from you: _____. Now ask yourself these questions, and check your honest response.

	yes	no
Am I willing to listen?	☐ yes	☐ no
Do I have the wisdom to help?	☐ yes	☐ no
Have I earned the person's trust?	☐ yes	☐ no

God is like a TOWER

The name of the Lord is a strong tower; the righteous run to it and are safe. Proverbs 18:10

You've seen a million pictures of the Eiffel Tower in France. But until you stand in front of it, you have no idea how huge it is, how beautiful it is, how amazing it is. No idea that this thing was built 40 years before an American skyscraper could surpass it in height. And you have no idea how breathtaking the view is from the top.

Now think. If the Eiffel Tower was built by Gustave Eiffel, and Gustave Eiffel was built by God, what kind of tower do you think *God* is?

ction shot   Read Psalm 61:2-3

Close-up

You are here

PENTATEUCH

OLD TESTAMENT

HISTORY

Job

PSALMS

Proverbs

POETRY

PROPHECY

NEW TESTAMENT

HISTORY

LETTERS

PROPHECY

In the passage you just read, what role does the tower play?

Circle the things that a tower does.

runs around   changes its mind   stands firm

takes vacations   doesn't change   provides shelter

becomes a landmark   provides protection   offers a view

Now which of the things you circled does God do for *you*? (Circle 'em again!)

Ramón's friends were pressuring him to steal things from a store. He refused to be a part of it—and kept on refusing, again and again. How was Ramón like a tower?

Cecilia helped a friend see a new perspective on her troubles. How was Cecilia like a tower?

A group of girls were saying really cruel things to Tina, and her friend Francie stood up for her. How was Francie like a tower?

Write about a time you were tower-like.

Print it!

What situation in your life could use a little more tower power right now? What can you do this week to stand tall, stand firm, provide shelter, or provide a view?

God is like a
CARPENTER

Unless the Lord builds the house, its builders labor in vain. Psalm 127:1

Carpenters don't start by swinging a hammer. In fact, that's just about the last thing they do. First they build the creation in their mind—what it will look like, what materials and tools they'll need. Then they gather the tools and materials they need. Finally, they're ready to start swinging a hammer.

God does the same thing with you. First he designs you—what you'll look like, what gifts you'll have, what personality type you'll be. Next he gathers up the tools and materials he'll need to make it happen. Then he gets to work. He starts on the project before you're born, and he works on it throughout your entire life.

ction shot | Read Philippians 1:6

Close-up

What's one thing God built into you that's totally cool?

Which of God's building projects do you think are the coolest? (You can only check three!)

- ☐ you!
- ☐ the moon
- ☐ animals
- ☐ people
- ☐ the earth
- ☐ planets
- ☐ plants
- ☐ heaven

You are here

PENTATEUCH

OLD TESTAMENT

HISTORY

POETRY

PROPHECY

NEW TESTAMENT

HISTORY

LETTERS

PROPHECY

Ephesians
PHILIPPIANS
Colossians

Did you know you inherited some of God's building ability? What's something you've made that you're proud of?

Draw a picture of something you'd like to build.

Okay, it's carpenter time. Think of a friendship that could use a little carpentry—you know, a relationship that needs a bit of work to improve it. Write a building plan.

Name of the project:

Tools I'll need:

The first thing I'll need to do:

Help I'll need:

How long I think it will take:

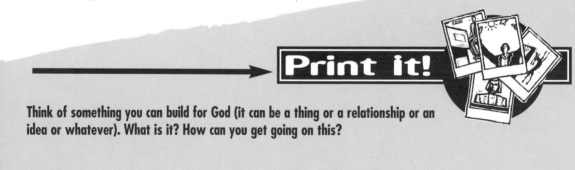

Print it!

Think of something you can build for God (it can be a thing or a relationship or an idea or whatever). What is it? How can you get going on this?

God is like an INVENTOR

You made the heavens, even the highest heavens, and all their starry host, the earth and all that is on it, the seas and all that is in them. Nehemiah 9:6

God made it all—think of it! And it's not like God had a bunch of other universes, earths, people, and animals to use as models. Before he made it all, there was absolutely nothing. He couldn't look at someone else's ideas and improve them. No, God created everything out of nothing. The ultimate inventor. He's big-time creative, inventing bats, jellyfish, caves, tidal waves, and *you*. You are his ultimate creation!

ction Shot

Read Genesis, chapter 1 (Yeah, the whole thing— don't be a wimp!)

Close-up

You are here

GENESIS
PENTATEUCH
Exodus
Leviticus

OLD TESTAMENT
HISTORY
POETRY
PROPHECY

NEW TESTAMENT
HISTORY
LETTERS
PROPHECY

The Nehemiah verse says that God made—
(Check all that are true.)

- ☐ the earth
- ☐ the common cold
- ☐ everything on the earth
- ☐ the heavens
- ☑ everything in the seas
- ☐ little brothers and sisters
- ☑ detention
- ☑ the highest heavens
- ☐ Rhode Island
- ☐ the seas
- ☐ powdered donuts

Besides humans, what do you think was God's coolest invention?

Why do you think God invented all this, especially you?

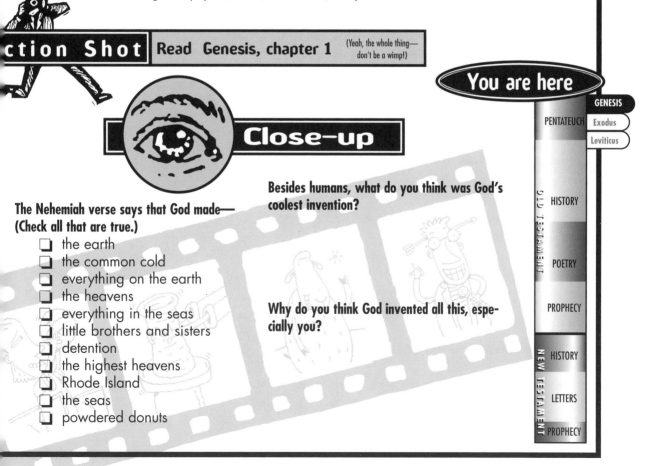

Draw an animal that doesn't exist, that you would invent if you could.

If you were to invent a *smulzenglubulator,* what would it be?

How can you use your creativity for God?

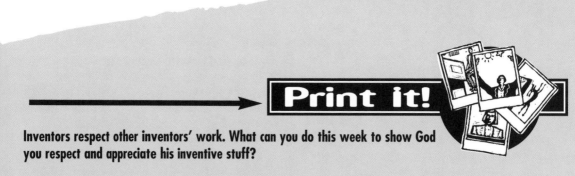

Print it!

Inventors respect other inventors' work. What can you do this week to show God you respect and appreciate his inventive stuff?

God is like an
EAGLE

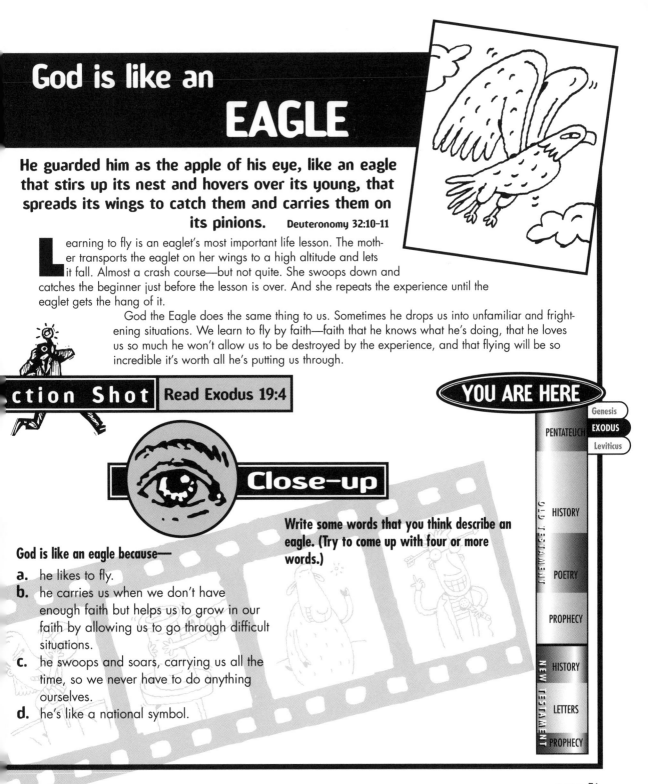

He guarded him as the apple of his eye, like an eagle that stirs up its nest and hovers over its young, that spreads its wings to catch them and carries them on its pinions. Deuteronomy 32:10-11

Learning to fly is an eaglet's most important life lesson. The mother transports the eaglet on her wings to a high altitude and lets it fall. Almost a crash course—but not quite. She swoops down and catches the beginner just before the lesson is over. And she repeats the experience until the eaglet gets the hang of it.

God the Eagle does the same thing to us. Sometimes he drops us into unfamiliar and frightening situations. We learn to fly by faith—faith that he knows what he's doing, that he loves us so much he won't allow us to be destroyed by the experience, and that flying will be so incredible it's worth all he's putting us through.

ction Shot | **Read Exodus 19:4**

Close-up

YOU ARE HERE

Genesis
PENTATEUCH **EXODUS**
Leviticus

OLD TESTAMENT
HISTORY
POETRY
PROPHECY

NEW TESTAMENT
HISTORY
LETTERS
PROPHECY

God is like an eagle because—

a. he likes to fly.

b. he carries us when we don't have enough faith but helps us to grow in our faith by allowing us to go through difficult situations.

c. he swoops and soars, carrying us all the time, so we never have to do anything ourselves.

d. he's like a national symbol.

Write some words that you think describe an eagle. (Try to come up with four or more words.)

Self-portrait

Which of these do you think is really Isaiah 40:31?

❏ But those who hope in the Lord will renew their strength. They will soar on wings like eagles; they will run and not grow weary, they will walk and not be faint.

❏ Yea, God is like an eagle; and so art thou. But woe to those who are careless, for they will end up stuffed and perched in someone's hunting lodge.

❏ *Eagle* rhymes with *beagle*, which almost sounds like *bugle*, which makes a loud, obnoxious sound.

If you got the right answer there, then you'll see that the Bible doesn't just describe God as an eagle—it says that with him, *we* can be like eagles, too! If you did what that Isaiah 40 verse says, what would you be doing?

What kind of bird do you feel like?

❏ an eagle ❏ a pterodactyl

❏ a pigeon ❏ a hummingbird

❏ a chicken ❏ an ostrich

Why?

Print it!

If you're going to continue to grow as an eagle, you'll need to continue your flying lessons with God. What's one area of your life where you think God would like you to stretch your wings in faith a bit more?

❏ sharing my faith with a friend ❏ moving away from a bad habit

❏ fixing a bad relationship ❏ other:_____

God is like a
SERVANT

Here is my servant, whom I uphold, my chosen one in whom I delight; I will put my Spirit on him and he will bring justice to the nations. Isaiah 42:1

All governments and companies around the world and in all times have developed organizational charts with the head honcho at the top—queen, president, dictator, kahuna, grand pooh-bah—and with lesser honchos arranged at various levels beneath the head honcho. Along comes Jesus, who flips the whole thing upside down. The first will be last, the high and mighty will be humbled…all sorts of radical stuff like that. And Jesus didn't just stand in a pulpit and preach about servanthood—he got down on his hands and knees and washed people's feet.

ction Shot | Read Philippians 2:6-7

You are here

Close-up

Use the letters in the word *SERVANT* to make an acrostic that describes a servant. In other words *S* could stand for "Selfish? No way!"

S
E
R
V
A
N
T

What's so amazing about the fact that Jesus served people? (*Hint:* remember who he is.)

PENTATEUCH

HISTORY

OLD TESTAMENT

POETRY

PROPHECY

HISTORY

NEW TESTAMENT

LETTERS

PROPHECY

Ephesians
PHILIPPIANS
Colossians

Write a short story about a junior higher who was a great servant.

Why is it so difficult to serve people? (Circle all that are true for you—*be really honest!*)

I'm selfish.

It means I have to think about other people.

It's inconvenient.

I don't usually think of it.

I don't feel like it.

I don't get anything for it.

I'd rather have them serve me.

I don't know.

Name one or two ways you served someone in the last week.

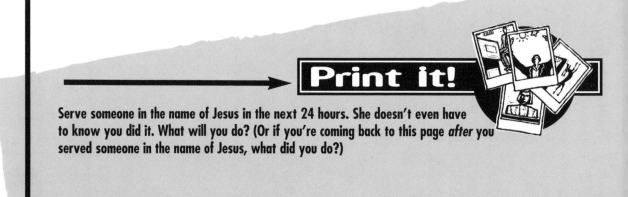

Print it!

Serve someone in the name of Jesus in the next 24 hours. She doesn't even have to know you did it. What will you do? (Or if you're coming back to this page *after* you served someone in the name of Jesus, what did you do?)

God is like a
BiG SiSTER or BROTHER

Whoever does God's will is my brother and sister and mother. Mark 3:35

If they're good, big brothers and sisters watch out for you. They don't make your life perfect, but it's good to know they're around, just in case you need someone to protect you against a bully.

Jesus is like that. Life has its share of scraped knees and bloodied noses, but there's real comfort knowing that he's there, ready to step in if things turn nasty. And it's bad news for anyone he catches messing with *his* kid brothers and sisters.

Action Shot   Read 1 John 3:1

You are here

Close-up

If Jesus is God's Son, and you're a child of God, then what's the relationship between you and Jesus?

How can this older brother help you?

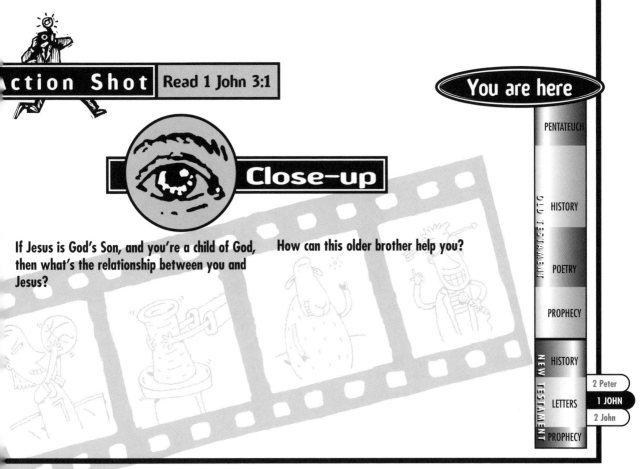

PENTATEUCH

OLD TESTAMENT

HISTORY

POETRY

PROPHECY

NEW TESTAMENT

HISTORY

LETTERS

PROPHECY

2 Peter

1 JOHN

2 John

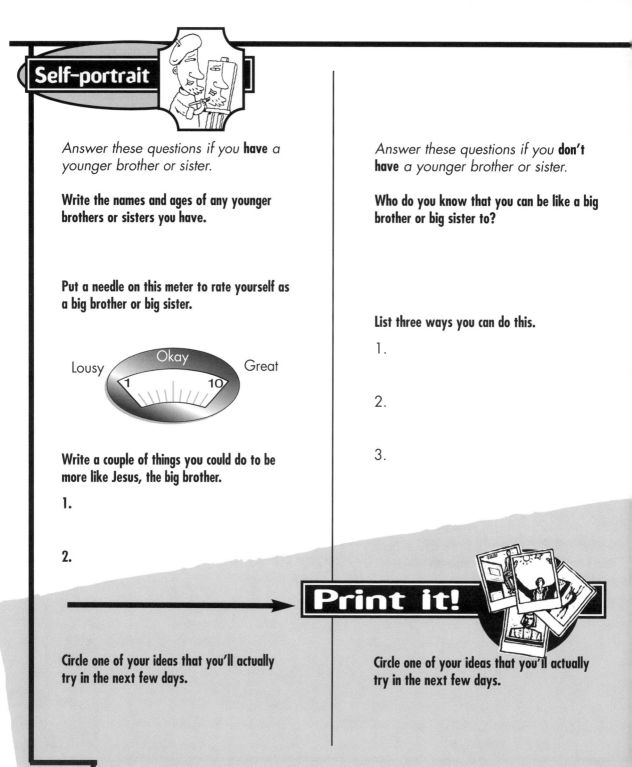

*Answer these questions if you **have** a younger brother or sister.*

Write the names and ages of any younger brothers or sisters you have.

Put a needle on this meter to rate yourself as a big brother or big sister.

Lousy   Okay   Great

1   10

Write a couple of things you could do to be more like Jesus, the big brother.

1.

2.

*Answer these questions if you **don't have** a younger brother or sister.*

Who do you know that you can be like a big brother or big sister to?

List three ways you can do this.

1.

2.

3.

Print it!

Circle one of your ideas that you'll actually try in the next few days.

Circle one of your ideas that you'll actually try in the next few days.

God is like a
SHiELD

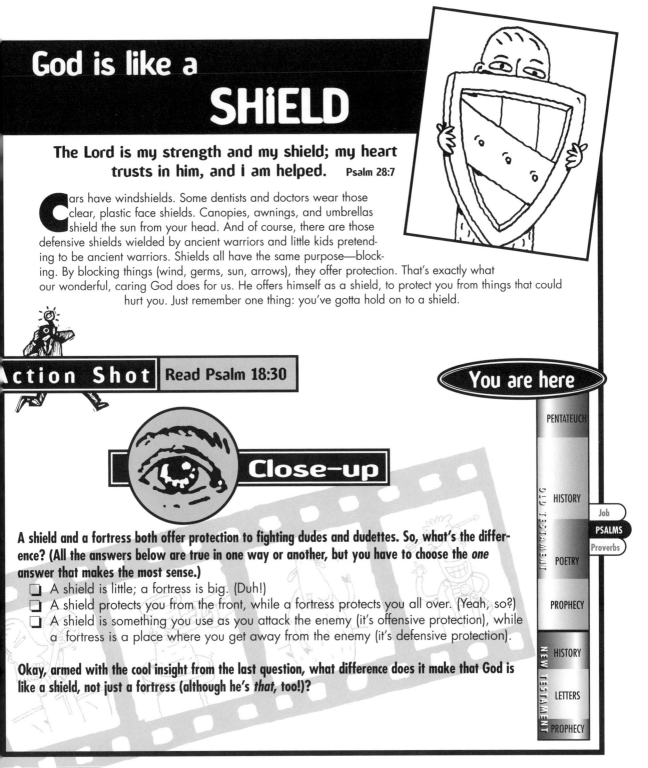

The Lord is my strength and my shield; my heart trusts in him, and I am helped. Psalm 28:7

Cars have windshields. Some dentists and doctors wear those clear, plastic face shields. Canopies, awnings, and umbrellas shield the sun from your head. And of course, there are those defensive shields wielded by ancient warriors and little kids pretending to be ancient warriors. Shields all have the same purpose—blocking. By blocking things (wind, germs, sun, arrows), they offer protection. That's exactly what our wonderful, caring God does for us. He offers himself as a shield, to protect you from things that could hurt you. Just remember one thing: you've gotta hold on to a shield.

Action Shot | Read Psalm 18:30

Close-up

A shield and a fortress both offer protection to fighting dudes and dudettes. So, what's the difference? (All the answers below are true in one way or another, but you have to choose the *one* answer that makes the most sense.)

- ☐ A shield is little; a fortress is big. (Duh!)
- ☐ A shield protects you from the front, while a fortress protects you all over. (Yeah, so?)
- ☐ A shield is something you use as you attack the enemy (it's offensive protection), while a fortress is a place where you get away from the enemy (it's defensive protection).

Okay, armed with the cool insight from the last question, what difference does it make that God is like a shield, not just a fortress (although he's *that*, too!)?

You are here

PENTATEUCH

OLD TESTAMENT

HISTORY

Job
PSALMS
Proverbs

POETRY

PROPHECY

NEW TESTAMENT

HISTORY

LETTERS

PROPHECY

Self-portrait

Amy's friends are picking on Tina. You know how groups can be mean to someone for no reason at all. Well, poor Tina's hardly got any friends, and now there are girls calling her names and talking behind her back. How can Amy be a shield for Tina?

Fernando's in eighth grade, and his little sister's in sixth grade, so she's in the same middle school with him. She's not a bad sister, but Fernando's still kind of embarrassed about her. At the same time Nando feels bad for her because she's having a tough time fitting in at this school. How can Nando be a shield for his little sister?

List at least three ways that a young teen can be a shield for someone else (and you can't just say "protect him").

1.

2.

3.

Print it!

Who will you whip out your shield-ability for this week? When and where will you do it?

God is like a
JEALOUS LOVER

Do not worship any other god, for the Lord, whose name is Jealous, is a jealous God. **Exodus 34:14**

The whole Bible is a story of God the Jealous Lover. He loves us; we run away. He pursues us; we take off again. He forgives and comes after us; we ignore him and focus on ourselves. God is a jealous lover. He hates it when we set him aside to pursue other loves. After all, he's sworn himself to be *our* lover. As our lover, he's chosen to carry out his dreams through us. If we intend to be faithful, we've got to live our dreams through him.

ction Shot | Read Deuteronomy 4:24

Close-up

How do you think you would feel if you were in love and the object of your affection was flirting with other people? (Circle all the words you think you'd feel.)

happy

MAD

carefree

jealous

vengeful

depressed

hungry

desperate

frantic

What's a jealous lover?

❏ A lover who doesn't want to share the object of his affection with anyone or anything.

❏ A lover who stalks the object of his affection and is always suspicious that she's not being faithful.

❏ A lover only interested in her own needs and desires.

Now put it in your own words. Why does God use this picture to describe himself?

You are here

PENTATEUCH | Numbers | **DEUTERONOMY** | Joshua

OLD TESTAMENT

HISTORY

POETRY

PROPHECY

NEW TESTAMENT

HISTORY

LETTERS

PROPHECY

Self-portrait

What things or people in your life do you really, really care about—enough to be jealous if they were threatened or taken away?

When is it good to be jealous? When is it *not* so good to be jealous?

Okay, God's jealousy is cool, because he's jealous for *you!* So what would jealousy for God look like on your part? (Yeah, it's a hard question—but give it some thought. Here's a hint: you don't have to worry about God's attention being turned away from you, so your jealousy would have to be the result of some other threat to your relationship with him.)

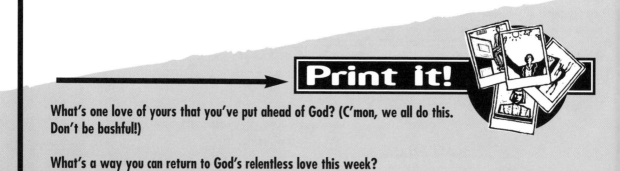

Print it!

What's one love of yours that you've put ahead of God? (C'mon, we all do this. Don't be bashful!)

What's a way you can return to God's relentless love this week?

God is like a
DAD

How great is the love the Father has lavished on us, that we should be called children of God! And that is what we are! 1 John 3:1

This God-picture is probably one of the most familiar. That makes it kinda hard because that means you already have a bunch of ideas of what it means that God is like a dad. Some of those ideas are right on and good, and some of them are just plain messed up.

So start over again. Look at the Daddy God picture for the first time, again, today. And just maybe he'll surprise you with his big, strong, loving arms of security.

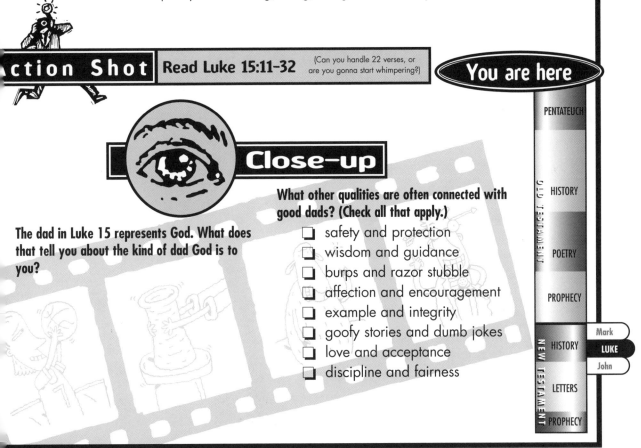

ction Shot   **Read Luke 15:11–32**   (Can you handle 22 verses, or are you gonna start whimpering?)

You are here

Close-up

The dad in Luke 15 represents God. What does that tell you about the kind of dad God is to you?

What other qualities are often connected with good dads? (Check all that apply.)

- ❑ safety and protection
- ❑ wisdom and guidance
- ❑ burps and razor stubble
- ❑ affection and encouragement
- ❑ example and integrity
- ❑ goofy stories and dumb jokes
- ❑ love and acceptance
- ❑ discipline and fairness

PENTATEUCH

OLD TESTAMENT

HISTORY

POETRY

PROPHECY

NEW TESTAMENT

HISTORY

LETTERS

PROPHECY

Mark
LUKE
John

Look at the qualities you checked on the previous page. If those are characteristics of *some* dads here on earth, how much more do you think God the Perfect Dad must have all of those and more? (Fill in the tie meter on the right to show your answer.)

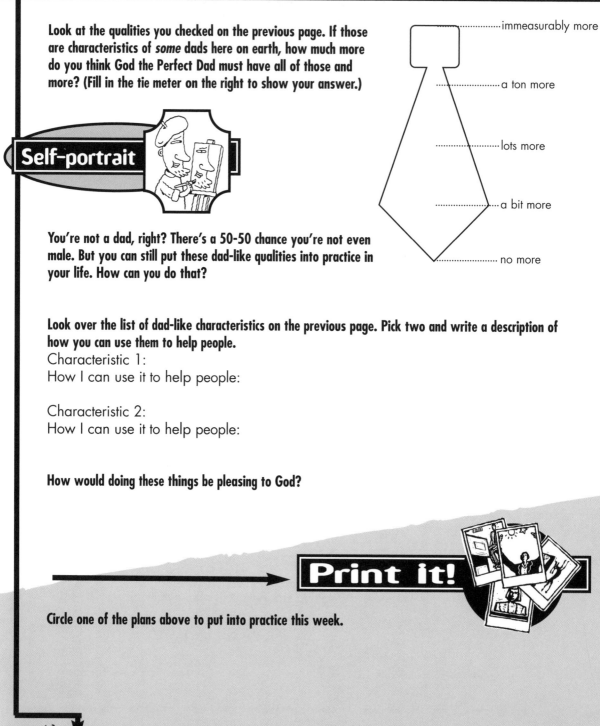

................immeasurably more

................a ton more

................lots more

................a bit more

.... no more

Self-portrait

You're not a dad, right? There's a 50-50 chance you're not even male. But you can still put these dad-like qualities into practice in your life. How can you do that?

Look over the list of dad-like characteristics on the previous page. Pick two and write a description of how you can use them to help people.

Characteristic 1:
How I can use it to help people:

Characteristic 2:
How I can use it to help people:

How would doing these things be pleasing to God?

Print it!

Circle one of the plans above to put into practice this week.

God is like a
LIFEGUARD

**He reached down from on high and took hold of me;
he drew me out of deep waters.**   2 Samuel 22:17

Lifeguards have two duties: the first is to *guard* you from danger; the second is to *save* you if you get into trouble. The first duty makes them post huge signs—NO HORSEPLAY (where did that word come from, anyway?)—and to yell, "No running on the pool deck!" If lifeguards didn't have the duty of guarding you from trouble, they'd be yelling things like, "Go ahead and run—I have a first aid kit!"

The second duty, to *save* you if you get into trouble, is just as important. It's their job to rescue you—even when you've ignored their advice by playing with horses or slipping while running. ("I *told* you not to run—now you'll have to lie there and bleed to death.")

Lifeguard God performs these same two duties all the time. He not only guards us from all sorts of hazards, but comes to save us when we get into trouble.

ction Shot | Read Psalm 69:14

Close-up

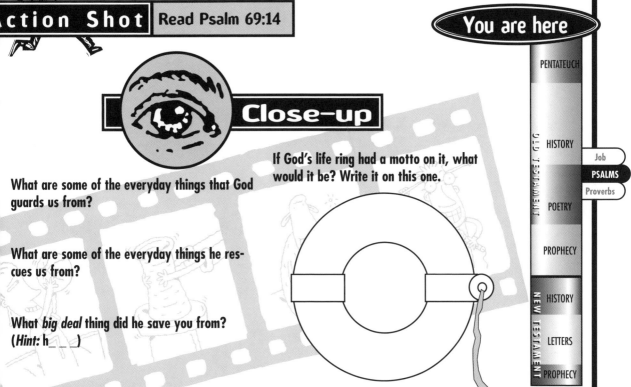

What are some of the everyday things that God guards us from?

What are some of the everyday things he rescues us from?

What *big deal* thing did he save you from? (*Hint:* h_ _ _)

If God's life ring had a motto on it, what would it be? Write it on this one.

You are here

PENTATEUCH

OLD TESTAMENT

HISTORY

Job
PSALMS
Proverbs

POETRY

PROPHECY

NEW TESTAMENT

HISTORY

LETTERS

PROPHECY

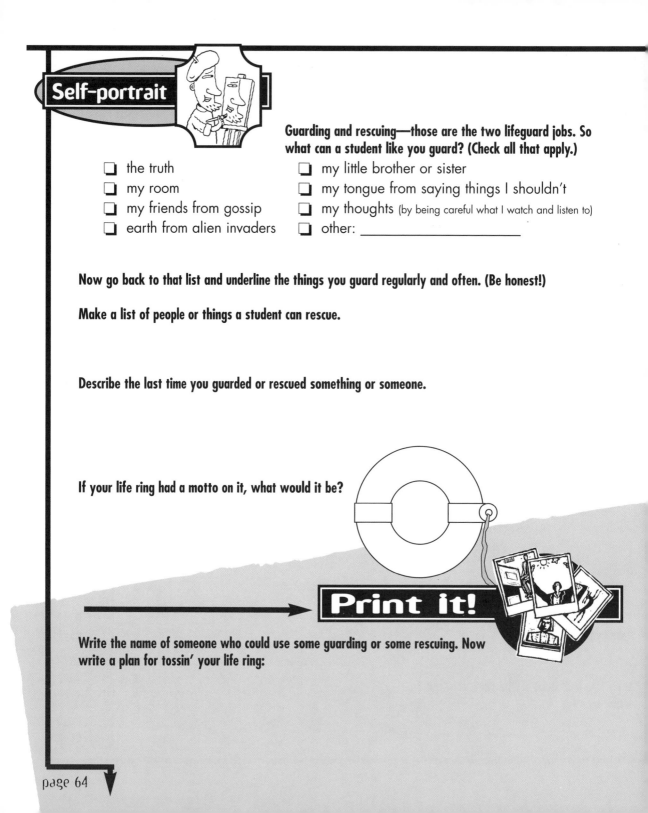

Guarding and rescuing—those are the two lifeguard jobs. So what can a student like you guard? (Check all that apply.)

❑ the truth
❑ my room
❑ my friends from gossip
❑ earth from alien invaders

❑ my little brother or sister
❑ my tongue from saying things I shouldn't
❑ my thoughts (by being careful what I watch and listen to)
❑ other: _____

Now go back to that list and underline the things you guard regularly and often. (Be honest!)

Make a list of people or things a student can rescue.

Describe the last time you guarded or rescued something or someone.

If your life ring had a motto on it, what would it be?

Print it!

Write the name of someone who could use some guarding or some rescuing. Now write a plan for tossin' your life ring:

God is like a FORT

The Lord is a refuge for the oppressed, a stronghold in times of trouble. Psalm 9:9

Y ou've built a fort, right? Every kid has. Yours might have been a temporary, low-budget model made with couch cushions and blankets. Or it might have been a deluxe version in a tree, complete with rope ladder and carpeting. At least your own room has probably become a fort for you—a place to get away from others, a place of privacy. Forts are cool places of protection, safety, and security. And that's exactly what God can be for you.

** action Shot** Read Psalm 32:7 and 59:16

Close-up

What does God (pictured as a fort) provide in these two passages?

Which of these sentences is most true for you?
- ☐ God's like a fort to me because he gives me security in life—I always know he's watching out for me.
- ☐ God's like a fort to me because I can run to him when I'm in trouble.
- ☐ God's like a fort to me because— um...well, if I'm totally honest, I don't really think of him as a fort to me.

You are here

PENTATEUCH

OLD TESTAMENT

HISTORY

Job

PSALMS

Proverbs

POETRY

PROPHECY

NEW TESTAMENT

HISTORY

LETTERS

PROPHECY

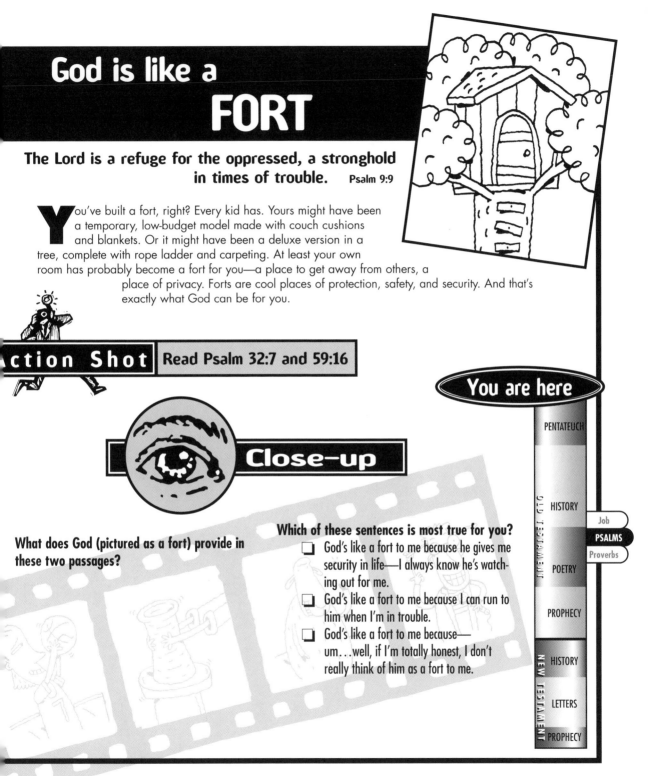

Have you ever been to an actual fort (like an old army fort or even one at Disneyland or somewhere)?

❑ Yes ❑ No

If yes, what was it like?

Describe one of the forts you've built. (If you can't remember any forts you've built, describe how your room is kind of like a fort.)

What's the best thing about forts?

How can you be like a fort to other people? (Look back at the previous page to see what it means for God to be like a fort.)

Print it!

Finish this sentence: I'm going to make someone feel safe this week by—

God is like an
HEiR

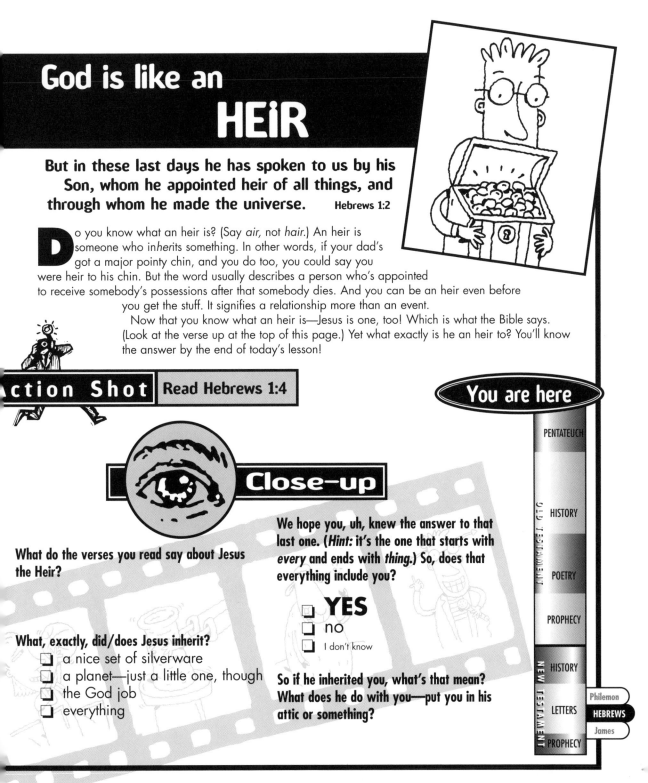

But in these last days he has spoken to us by his Son, whom he appointed heir of all things, and through whom he made the universe. Hebrews 1:2

Do you know what an heir is? (Say *air,* not *hair.*) An heir is someone who in*her*its something. In other words, if your dad's got a major pointy chin, and you do too, you could say you were heir to his chin. But the word usually describes a person who's appointed to receive somebody's possessions after that somebody dies. And you can be an heir even before you get the stuff. It signifies a relationship more than an event.

Now that you know what an heir is—Jesus is one, too! Which is what the Bible says. (Look at the verse up at the top of this page.) Yet what exactly is he an heir to? You'll know the answer by the end of today's lesson!

Action Shot — Read Hebrews 1:4

Close-up

What do the verses you read say about Jesus the Heir?

What, exactly, did/does Jesus inherit?
- ☐ a nice set of silverware
- ☐ a planet—just a little one, though
- ☐ the God job
- ☐ everything

We hope you, uh, knew the answer to that last one. (*Hint:* it's the one that starts with *every* and ends with *thing.*) So, does that everything include you?

- ☐ **YES**
- ☐ no
- ☐ I don't know

So if he inherited you, what's that mean? What does he do with you—put you in his attic or something?

You are here

OLD TESTAMENT
- PENTATEUCH
- HISTORY
- POETRY
- PROPHECY

NEW TESTAMENT
- HISTORY
- LETTERS — Philemon / **HEBREWS** / James
- PROPHECY

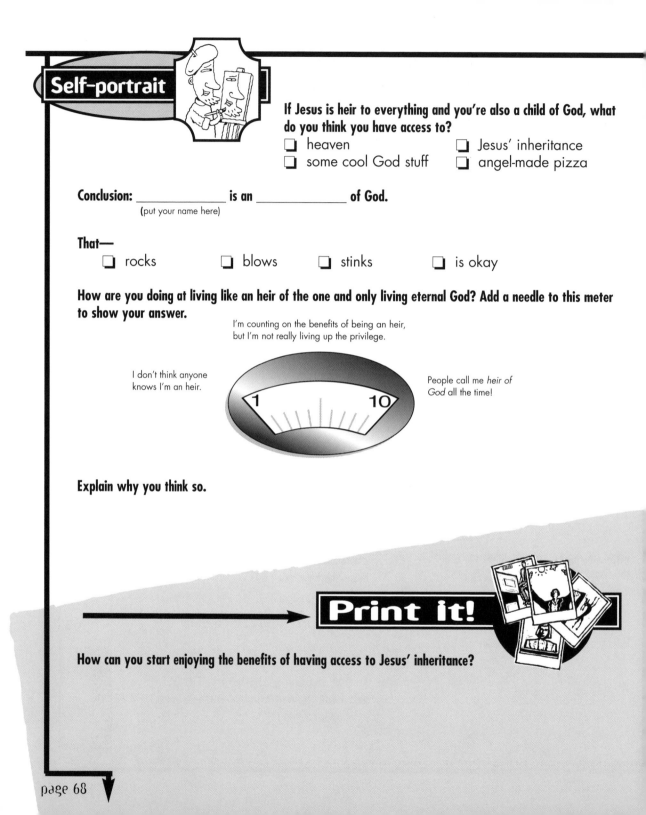
If Jesus is heir to everything and you're also a child of God, what do you think you have access to?

- ❏ heaven
- ❏ some cool God stuff
- ❏ Jesus' inheritance
- ❏ angel-made pizza

Conclusion: _____ is an _____ of God.
(put your name here)

That—

- ❏ rocks
- ❏ blows
- ❏ stinks
- ❏ is okay

How are you doing at living like an heir of the one and only living eternal God? Add a needle to this meter to show your answer.

I'm counting on the benefits of being an heir, but I'm not really living up the privilege.

I don't think anyone knows I'm an heir.

People call me *heir of God* all the time!

1   10

Explain why you think so.

Print it!

How can you start enjoying the benefits of having access to Jesus' inheritance?

God is like a
POTTER

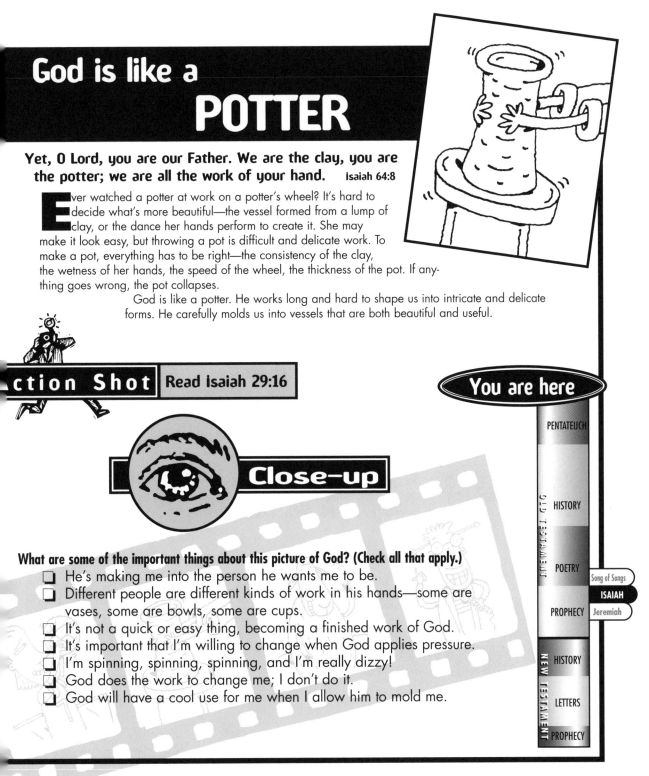

Yet, O Lord, you are our Father. We are the clay, you are the potter; we are all the work of your hand. Isaiah 64:8

Ever watched a potter at work on a potter's wheel? It's hard to decide what's more beautiful—the vessel formed from a lump of clay, or the dance her hands perform to create it. She may make it look easy, but throwing a pot is difficult and delicate work. To make a pot, everything has to be right—the consistency of the clay, the wetness of her hands, the speed of the wheel, the thickness of the pot. If anything goes wrong, the pot collapses.

God is like a potter. He works long and hard to shape us into intricate and delicate forms. He carefully molds us into vessels that are both beautiful and useful.

ction Shot Read Isaiah 29:16

Close-up

You are here

What are some of the important things about this picture of God? (Check all that apply.)

- ❏ He's making me into the person he wants me to be.
- ❏ Different people are different kinds of work in his hands—some are vases, some are bowls, some are cups.
- ❏ It's not a quick or easy thing, becoming a finished work of God.
- ❏ It's important that I'm willing to change when God applies pressure.
- ❏ I'm spinning, spinning, spinning, and I'm really dizzy!
- ❏ God does the work to change me; I don't do it.
- ❏ God will have a cool use for me when I allow him to mold me.

PENTATEUCH

OLD TESTAMENT

HISTORY

POETRY

Song of Songs

ISAIAH

PROPHECY

Jeremiah

NEW TESTAMENT

HISTORY

LETTERS

PROPHECY

Which of these clay things would you say represents what God might mold you into? (Circle one.)

Why'd you pick that one?

What would it mean for you to shape or mold something or someone?

Kenny has been playing basketball for a long time, and he's really good. His teammates totally look to him for direction and example. He decides he's going to take this shaping and molding seriously. What can Kenny do to have a shaping and molding influence for God on his team?

Jenna hangs out all the time with Kristi, who's constantly trying to get attention. In fact Kristi will do just about anything for attention, including going along with the crowd or saying things just to shock people. What can Jenna do to have a shaping and molding influence on Kristi?

Print it!

Sure, it's actually God who does the shaping and molding, not you. But you can be a tool in God's hand to help shape and mold someone. How can you put yourself in the place this week where God can use you as a tool to shape and mold someone?

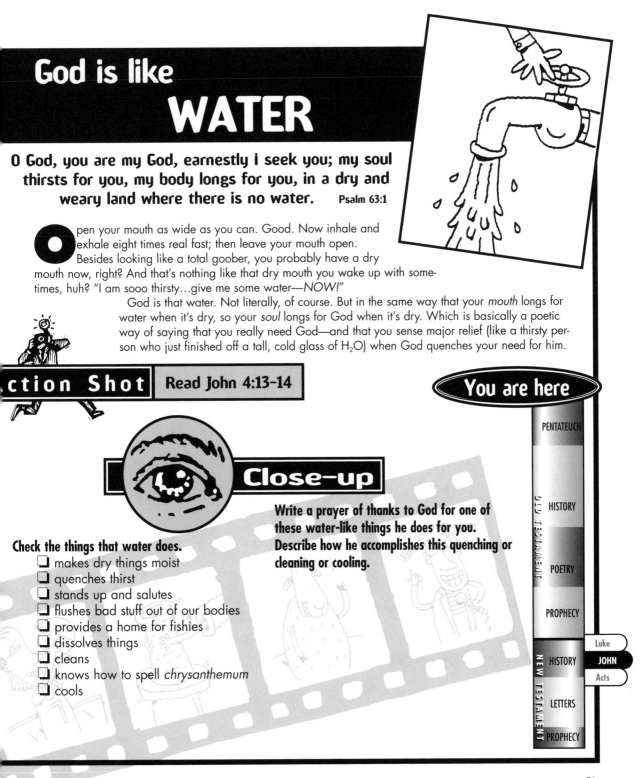

God is like
WATER

O God, you are my God, earnestly I seek you; my soul thirsts for you, my body longs for you, in a dry and weary land where there is no water. Psalm 63:1

Open your mouth as wide as you can. Good. Now inhale and exhale eight times real fast; then leave your mouth open. Besides looking like a total goober, you probably have a dry mouth now, right? And that's nothing like that dry mouth you wake up with sometimes, huh? "I am sooo thirsty…give me some water—*NOW!*"

God is that water. Not literally, of course. But in the same way that your *mouth* longs for water when it's dry, so your *soul* longs for God when it's dry. Which is basically a poetic way of saying that you really need God—and that you sense major relief (like a thirsty person who just finished off a tall, cold glass of H_2O) when God quenches your need for him.

ction Shot Read John 4:13–14

You are here

Close-up

Write a prayer of thanks to God for one of these water-like things he does for you. Describe how he accomplishes this quenching or cleaning or cooling.

Check the things that water does.
- ❑ makes dry things moist
- ❑ quenches thirst
- ❑ stands up and salutes
- ❑ flushes bad stuff out of our bodies
- ❑ provides a home for fishies
- ❑ dissolves things
- ❑ cleans
- ❑ knows how to spell *chrysanthemum*
- ❑ cools

PENTATEUCH

OLD TESTAMENT

HISTORY

POETRY

PROPHECY

NEW TESTAMENT

HISTORY

Luke
JOHN
Acts

LETTERS

PROPHECY

How do you use water? (Check all that apply.)

- ❏ cleaning my armpits
- ❏ drinking
- ❏ having water-balloon fights
- ❏ cooking my veggies
- ❏ diving and swimming
- ❏ watering my plants
- ❏ gargling
- ❏ cooling off my sweaty face
- ❏ washing my mom's car
- ❏ making Kool-Aid
- ❏ keeping me alive

- ❏ washing my ketchup-crusted dishes
- ❏ providing me with drool and spit
- ❏ cradling my rubber duckie
- ❏ mesmerizing me as I stare at a waterfall
- ❏ running through as it's coming out the sprinkler
- ❏ pouring into my dad's steaming car radiator
- ❏ pretending I'm a fountain and spitting it in the air
- ❏ holding up my canoe or sailboat or motorboat

How are you like water to other people? (Check 'em!)

- ❏ When I forgive, instead of getting even with people, I extinguish a fiery situation.
- ❏ When I'm nice to lonely kids, I quench their need to know someone cares about them.
- ❏ When I challenge a friend to move away from some wrong behavior in his life, I'm part of a cleaning process.
- ❏ When I serve older people and treat them with respect, I am refreshing.
- ❏ When I obey my parents with a great attitude, I refresh them like a fun water fight.
- ❏ When I serve people without looking for something in return, I *rehydrate* them.
- ❏ When I worship God, I'm actually like water to him, satisfying his desire for me to focus on him.
- ❏ When I'm friendly to the lonely person on my street, I help dissolve her hard and angry heart.

Print it!

Write a water plan. Decide how you'll try to be like water to someone this week. How will you put this God-quality into practice?

God is like
BREAD

i am the bread of life. John 6:48

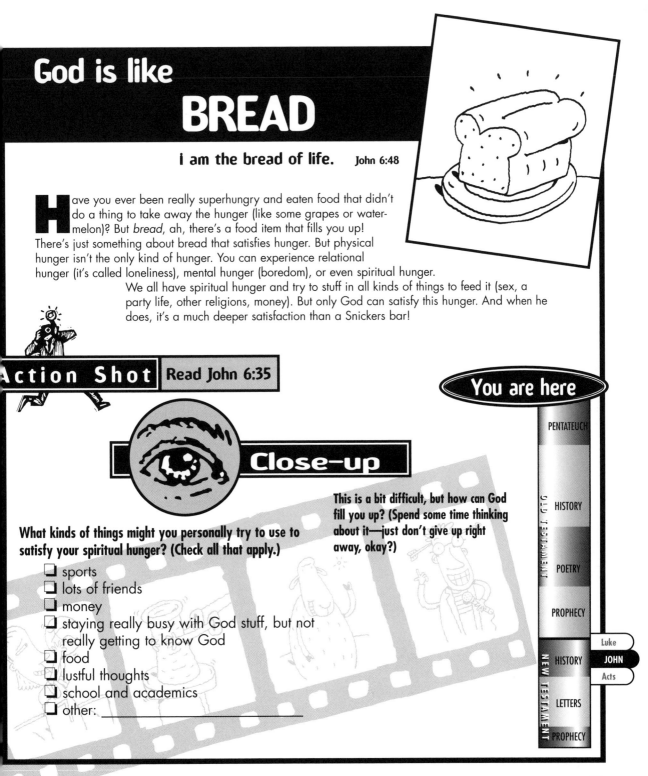

Have you ever been really superhungry and eaten food that didn't do a thing to take away the hunger (like some grapes or watermelon)? But *bread*, ah, there's a food item that fills you up! There's just something about bread that satisfies hunger. But physical hunger isn't the only kind of hunger. You can experience relational hunger (it's called loneliness), mental hunger (boredom), or even spiritual hunger.

We all have spiritual hunger and try to stuff in all kinds of things to feed it (sex, a party life, other religions, money). But only God can satisfy this hunger. And when he does, it's a much deeper satisfaction than a Snickers bar!

Action Shot | Read John 6:35

Close-up

What kinds of things might you personally try to use to satisfy your spiritual hunger? (Check all that apply.)

- ☐ sports
- ☐ lots of friends
- ☐ money
- ☐ staying really busy with God stuff, but not really getting to know God
- ☐ food
- ☐ lustful thoughts
- ☐ school and academics
- ☐ other: _____

This is a bit difficult, but how can God fill you up? (Spend some time thinking about it—just don't give up right away, okay?)

You are here

PENTATEUCH

OLD TESTAMENT

HISTORY

POETRY

PROPHECY

Luke

JOHN

Acts

NEW TESTAMENT

HISTORY

LETTERS

PROPHECY

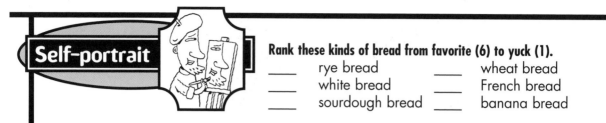

Rank these kinds of bread from favorite (6) to yuck (1).

____	rye bread	____	wheat bread
____	white bread	____	French bread
____	sourdough bread	____	banana bread

Okay, since God is like bread—he fills your spiritual need—how can *you* be like bread to someone else?

Which of these students is the most like bread—Karen, Alex, or Meesha? Which is the second most? Which is the least? (Write a big 1, 2, and 3 right on top of them.)

Karen sees a girl in her lunchroom who's sitting all alone. Even though she doesn't know her, Karen sits by her and starts a conversation.

Alex has a friend who's really into horoscopes. His friend said it gives him some direction in life. Alex answered, "I can think of something better than that."

Meesha's mom is tired all the time from working two jobs and taking care of their home. Meesha thinks about helping more, but decides she doesn't want to.

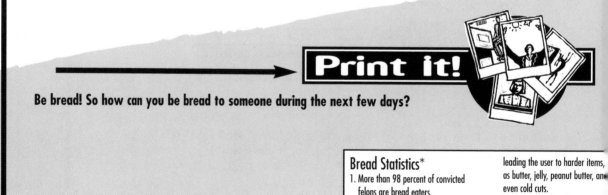

Print it!

Be bread! So how can you be bread to someone during the next few days?

Bread Statistics*

1. More than 98 percent of convicted felons are bread eaters.
2. Fully *half* of all children who grow up in bread-consuming households score below average on standardized tests.
3. More than 90 percent of violent crimes are committed within 24 hours of eating bread.
4. Bread has been proven to be addictive. Subjects deprived of bread and given only water to eat actually begged for bread after only two days.
5. Bread is often a gateway food item, leading the user to harder items, as butter, jelly, peanut butter, an even cold cuts.
6. Most American bread eaters are ly unable to distinguish between nificant scientific fact and meani statistical babbling.

*Collected from Fred "Gossip" Gustafson we know, who swears he heard these fr friend who said he read them in the Sea Herald. . .or maybe it was *The National Enquirer*. Or *Soap Opera Digest*. Well, it one of those.

God is like a
SHEPHERD

i am the good shepherd. The good shepherd lays down his life for the sheep. John 10:11

Pretty much everyone's familiar with God as a shepherd ("The Lord is my shepherd, I shall not want…"). But it's a lot more difficult to admit that *we're* sheep. It's not a flattering picture of ourselves. Sheep are stupid, easily frightened, and always wandering into trouble. And like most animals, they're preoccupied with feeding themselves. So we're sheep, huh? Ouch. At least there's some comfort in knowing that, if we're going to act like sheep, Jesus wants to be our shepherd.

ction Shot | Read Psalm 23:1

Close-up

What's a shepherd do, anyway?
- ❑ forgets about the sheep
- ❑ protects sheep
- ❑ leads sheep to rest
- ❑ helps sheep find food and water
- ❑ ignores the sheep
- ❑ helps sheep when they're sick or hurt

How does God do these things for you?

If you had to choose one word to sum up what a shepherd does, which of these would it be?
- ❑ care
- ❑ protect
- ❑ lead

You are here

PENTATEUCH

OLD TESTAMENT

HISTORY

Job

PSALMS

Proverbs

POETRY

PROPHECY

NEW TESTAMENT

HISTORY

LETTERS

PROPHECY

Self-portrait

Think of the word you picked for the last question. Circle some of the shepherd's staffs to rate yourself as to how well you do that thing (above) on a regular basis.

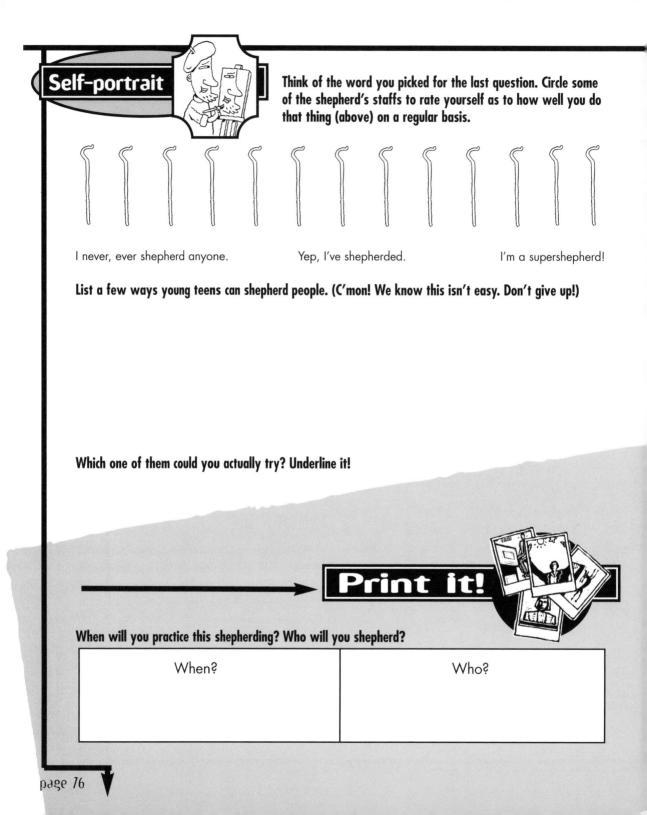

I never, ever shepherd anyone.   Yep, I've shepherded.   I'm a supershepherd!

List a few ways young teens can shepherd people. (C'mon! We know this isn't easy. Don't give up!)

Which one of them could you actually try? Underline it!

Print it!

When will you practice this shepherding? Who will you shepherd?

When?	Who?

God is like a
TEAM CAPTAIN

But you are a chosen people, a royal priesthood, a holy nation, a people belonging to God, that you may declare the praises of him who called you out of darkness into his wonderful light. 1 Peter 2:9

The Bible says that God chooses you to be on his team. Remember those elementary school days at recess or in P.E., where you were one of a bunch of kids being slowly, painfully, chosen one by one to be on a team? And you sweated it out, wondering if you'd ever get chosen. You may wonder why *God* picks you. Maybe you think he chooses you because he *has* to. ("Oh well, I'm *supposed* to pick her. I am God, after all—and besides, it's in my contract.") Or maybe you think he picks you because he feels sorry for you. ("I'd better choose him, because if I don't, nobody will.") But no, Team Captain God chooses you because he *wants* to. He wants *you* on his team.

ction Shot | Read Colossians 3:12

Close-up

What did God choose you _for_?

How would your life be different if you'd weaseled your way onto God's team, instead of being chosen?

You are here

PENTATEUCH

OLD TESTAMENT

HISTORY

POETRY

PROPHECY

NEW TESTAMENT

HISTORY

LETTERS

PROPHECY

Philippians
COLOSSIANS
1 Thessalonians

Self-portrait

God the Team Captain chose you. How can you help other people see that he wants to choose them, too?

What's the difference between being *inclusive* and being *exclusive*?
- **a.** *Inclusive* starts with an *i*, and *exclusive* doesn't.
- **b.** Being inclusive means that you're part of something, while being exclusive means you're not part of it.
- **c.** Being inclusive means that you want to include people, while being exclusive means that you only include *certain* people.

Did you get the right answer to that last one? (Here's a big hint: the right answer *isn't* a or b.) So how can you, as a middle schooler, be inclusive?

Print it!

Name someone who could really benefit from being included in something. What could you do to include this person this week?

God is like a
BEST FRIEND

Greater love has no one than this, that he lay down his life for his friends. John 15:13

God is my best friend? Sounds like a nice thought; but really, is this idea anything more than something youth leaders and pastors say? I mean, is it real? Those are great questions, and you don't have to be embarrassed to ask them. But here's the deal: best friendships are two-way. In other words, you can't be best friends with someone if she doesn't feel the same way. God totally wants to be best friends with you. The question is this: do you want to be best friends with him?

Action Shot | Read John 15:15

Close-up

In this verse, Jesus says we *used* to be called—
- ❏ robots
- ❏ servants

But *now* we're called—
- ❏ friends
- ❏ boneheads

And the proof he offers for this is—
- ❏ I learned your secret handshake.
- ❏ I've told you everything.

A superimportant thing about best friends is that they let each other know all about themselves. What difference does it make to you that Jesus does this for you?

You are here

PENTATEUCH

OLD TESTAMENT

HISTORY

POETRY

PROPHECY

Luke

JOHN

Acts

NEW TESTAMENT

HISTORY

LETTERS

PROPHECY

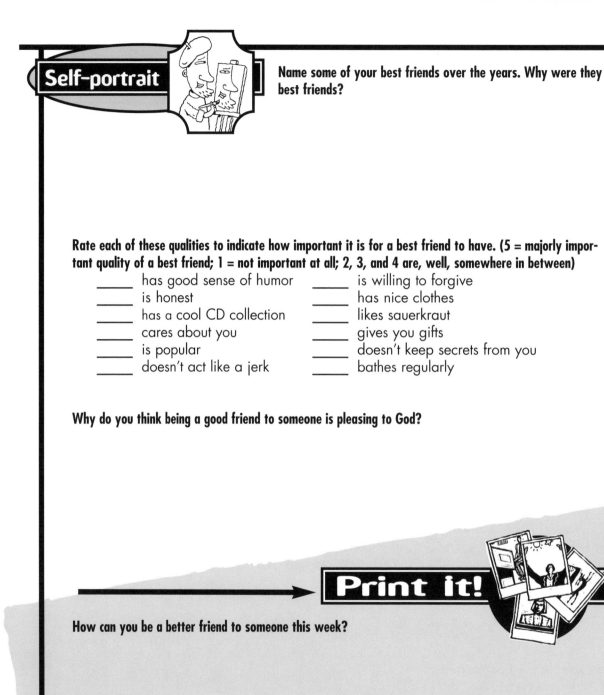

Self-portrait

Name some of your best friends over the years. Why were they best friends?

Rate each of these qualities to indicate how important it is for a best friend to have. (5 = majorly important quality of a best friend; 1 = not important at all; 2, 3, and 4 are, well, somewhere in between)

_____ has good sense of humor   _____ is willing to forgive
_____ is honest   _____ has nice clothes
_____ has a cool CD collection   _____ likes sauerkraut
_____ cares about you   _____ gives you gifts
_____ is popular   _____ doesn't keep secrets from you
_____ doesn't act like a jerk   _____ bathes regularly

Why do you think being a good friend to someone is pleasing to God?

Print it!

How can you be a better friend to someone this week?

God is like a
LiON

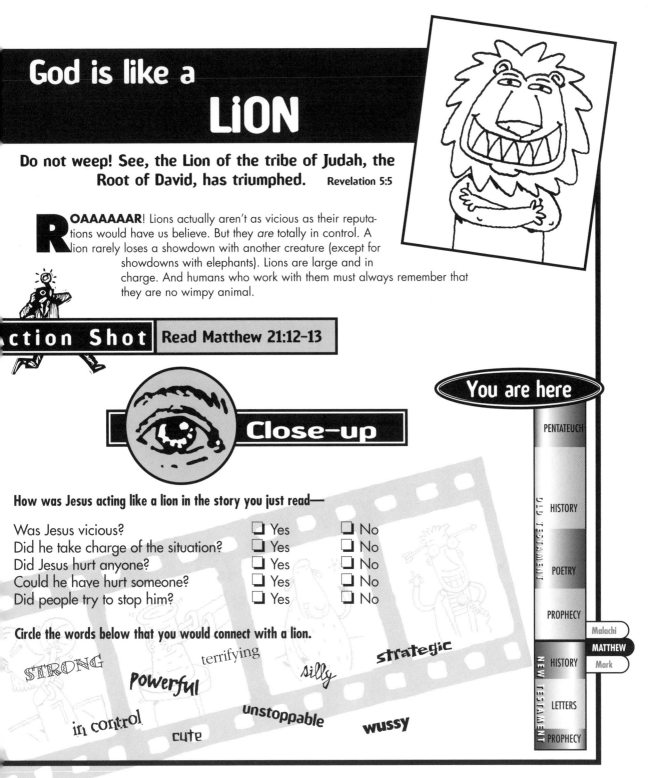

Do not weep! See, the Lion of the tribe of Judah, the Root of David, has triumphed. Revelation 5:5

ROAAAAAAR! Lions actually aren't as vicious as their reputations would have us believe. But they *are* totally in control. A lion rarely loses a showdown with another creature (except for showdowns with elephants). Lions are large and in charge. And humans who work with them must always remember that they are no wimpy animal.

ction Shot | Read Matthew 21:12–13

Close-up

You are here

PENTATEUCH

HISTORY

POETRY

PROPHECY

Malachi

MATTHEW

HISTORY

Mark

LETTERS

PROPHECY

OLD TESTAMENT

NEW TESTAMENT

How was Jesus acting like a lion in the story you just read—

Was Jesus vicious? ☐ Yes ☐ No
Did he take charge of the situation? ☐ Yes ☐ No
Did Jesus hurt anyone? ☐ Yes ☐ No
Could he have hurt someone? ☐ Yes ☐ No
Did people try to stop him? ☐ Yes ☐ No

Circle the words below that you would connect with a lion.

STRONG   terrifying   strategic
powerful   silly
in control   unstoppable   wussy
cute

When was the last time you took charge of a situation that needed some direction? What happened?

When was the last time you stood your ground and didn't give in, even though your friends tried to get you to change your mind? What happened?

Considering your answers to the above questions, what's your roar-factor? (How lion-like have you acted?)

purrrr   Meeooow   GRRRRR   **ROAAAAAR!**

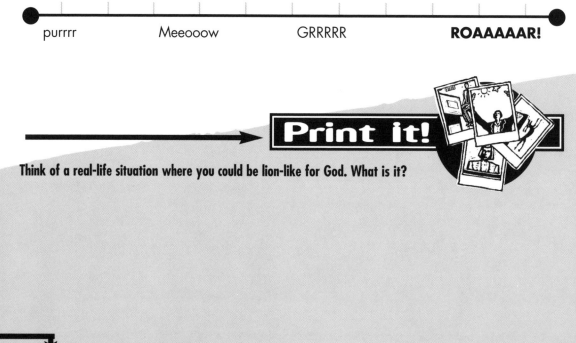

Print it!

Think of a real-life situation where you could be lion-like for God. What is it?

God is like a JUDGE

And the heavens proclaim his righteousness, for God himself is judge. Psalm 50:6

Getting to the truth is no simple task. Since God made us all unique, any two people witnessing the same thing are bound to see it differently. So a judge in a courtroom has to hear everyone's version and then try to determine what *really* happened. One of the reasons why Judge God is so fair is that he doesn't have to rely on the testimony of witnesses. He sees everything, so he knows all the facts. He also sees what's in our hearts, so he knows the motive behind every action. He knows the truth and judges us accordingly.

Action Shot — Read 2 Chronicles 19:7

Close-up

Which of these best describes what a judge is supposed to do?

a. sit behind an important looking bench, bang a wooden hammer, and say things like "Order!" and "I will hold you in contempt!"

b. listen to people present their arguments, then decide what's fair.

In what ways does God act like a judge?

How do you feel about this picture of God? Does he really seem like a fair judge?

The answer to the first question is b.

You are here

- PENTATEUCH
- OLD TESTAMENT
  - HISTORY
    - 1 Chronicles
    - 2 CHRONICLES
    - Ezra
  - POETRY
  - PROPHECY
- NEW TESTAMENT
  - HISTORY
  - LETTERS
  - PROPHECY

Self-portrait

You be the judge. Shantelle promised to come to Adam's party last Friday night, but she couldn't come at the last minute and she couldn't tell the reason why. They're mad at each other. Since they asked you for advice, what do you tell them?

Cole says that the teacher gave him a good grade because he gave her some money. You have a hard time believing this is true, but you're bugged by the idea that it might be. What do you do?

Think of two examples (they don't have to be real) of when a junior higher would need to act like a judge.

1.

2.

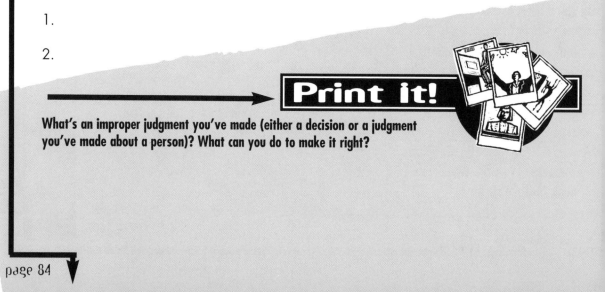

Print it!

What's an improper judgment you've made (either a decision or a judgment you've made about a person)? What can you do to make it right?

God is like a
PRiEST

For we do not have a high priest who is unable to sympathize with our weaknesses, but we have one who has been tempted in every way, just as we are—yet was without sin. Let us then approach the throne of grace with confidence. Hebrews 4:15-16

Hebrew priests offered the sacrifices on behalf of the Israelites. Then along comes Jesus. He's fully human, so he's qualified to speak for the human party; he's fully God, so he represents the heavenly realm—the perfect priest.

Here's a look at this new arrangement. You go to Jesus the Priest and confess your sin (that is, admit it, tell God you're sorry for disobeying him, and ask for forgiveness). As a fellow human, Jesus identifies with your struggle. He turns to the Father and says, "I know what she's done. I've made the payment for her sin, and I wish to forgive her." God says, "Do it." Then Jesus turns back to you and says, "Your sin is erased—you're forgiven." Now you're clean.

ction Shot | Read Hebrews 7:26-27

Close-up

Don't get hung up on whether your church has priests or pastors or ministers or whatever—that's not the issue here. The job of a priest in the Old Testament was to be a go-between from the people to God. And Jesus does that for us now.

When you go to Jesus to ask for forgiveness, how long does it take to get it?
- ☐ He has to process the right paperwork, so it can take a few days.
- ☐ He has to check with his Forgiveness Procedure Manual, which can take an hour or two.
- ☐ Duh, it's, like, right away.

When Jesus forgives your sins, what happens to them?
- ☐ They get stored in a sin container with your name on it.
- ☐ The Bible says they're separated from us as far as the east is from the west!

You are here

PENTATEUCH

OLD TESTAMENT

HISTORY

POETRY

PROPHECY

NEW TESTAMENT

HISTORY

LETTERS

PROPHECY

Philemon
HEBREWS
James

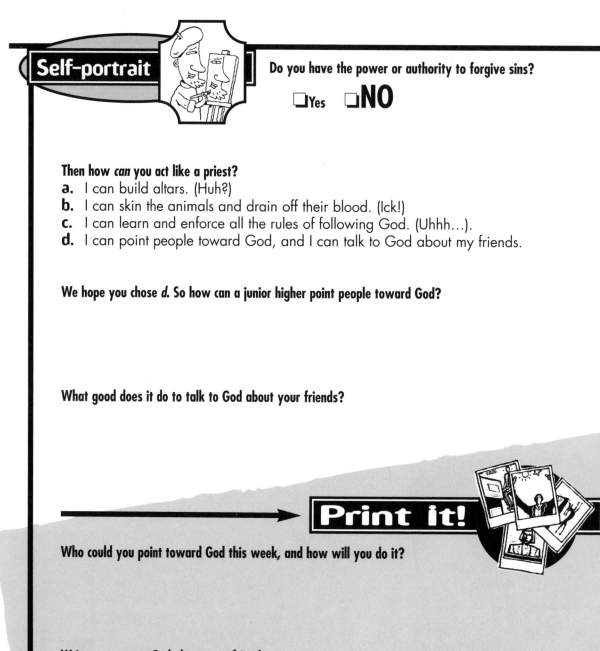

Do you have the power or authority to forgive sins?

❏Yes ❏**NO**

Then how *can* you act like a priest?
a. I can build altars. (Huh?)
b. I can skin the animals and drain off their blood. (Ick!)
c. I can learn and enforce all the rules of following God. (Uhhh…).
d. I can point people toward God, and I can talk to God about my friends.

We hope you chose *d*. So how can a junior higher point people toward God?

What good does it do to talk to God about your friends?

Print it!

Who could you point toward God this week, and how will you do it?

Write a prayer to God about your friend.

God is like a CHiLD

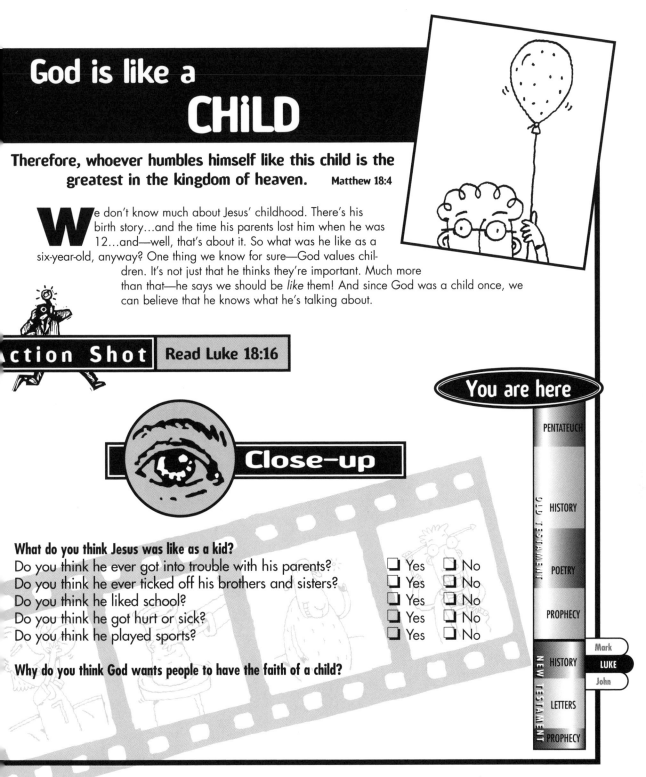

Therefore, whoever humbles himself like this child is the greatest in the kingdom of heaven. Matthew 18:4

We don't know much about Jesus' childhood. There's his birth story...and the time his parents lost him when he was 12...and—well, that's about it. So what was he like as a six-year-old, anyway? One thing we know for sure—God values children. It's not just that he thinks they're important. Much more than that—he says we should be *like* them! And since God was a child once, we can believe that he knows what he's talking about.

Action Shot | Read Luke 18:16

Close-up

What do you think Jesus was like as a kid?

Do you think he ever got into trouble with his parents?	☐ Yes	☐ No
Do you think he ever ticked off his brothers and sisters?	☐ Yes	☐ No
Do you think he liked school?	☐ Yes	☐ No
Do you think he got hurt or sick?	☐ Yes	☐ No
Do you think he played sports?	☐ Yes	☐ No

Why do you think God wants people to have the faith of a child?

You are here

PENTATEUCH

OLD TESTAMENT
HISTORY
POETRY
PROPHECY

NEW TESTAMENT
HISTORY
Mark
LUKE
John
LETTERS
PROPHECY

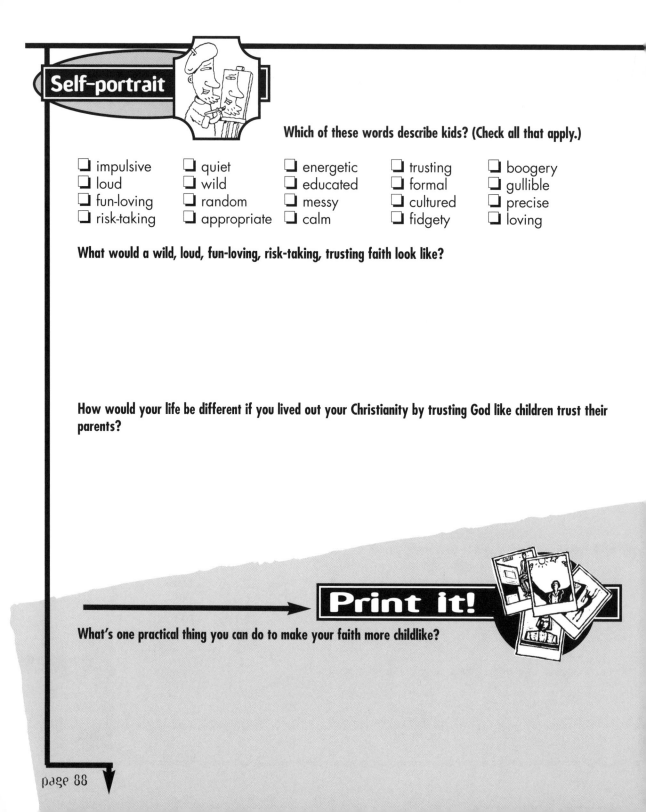
Which of these words describe kids? (Check all that apply.)

- ❏ impulsive
- ❏ loud
- ❏ fun-loving
- ❏ risk-taking

- ❏ quiet
- ❏ wild
- ❏ random
- ❏ appropriate

- ❏ energetic
- ❏ educated
- ❏ messy
- ❏ calm

- ❏ trusting
- ❏ formal
- ❏ cultured
- ❏ fidgety

- ❏ boogery
- ❏ gullible
- ❏ precise
- ❏ loving

What would a wild, loud, fun-loving, risk-taking, trusting faith look like?

How would your life be different if you lived out your Christianity by trusting God like children trust their parents?

Print it!

What's one practical thing you can do to make your faith more childlike?

God is like a CORNERSTONE

> See, I lay a stone in Zion, a tested stone, a precious cornerstone for a sure foundation; the one who trusts will never be dismayed. **Isaiah 28:16**

With most things in life, if you get off to a rough start, you can go back and fix it later. If you don't like the introduction to a story you're writing, you can finish the story, then go back and rewrite the opening. If you get a bad grade on the first test in a class, you can still pull off an A in the class by doing well on the other tests.

Not so when it comes to building stone walls. If you don't set that first stone straight and right, everything above it will always be crooked or unstable. That first stone—it's the cornerstone. And it's the most important part of the foundation.

Action Shot | Read Ephesians 2:20

Close-up

What's the difference between a cornerstone and a foundation?

How is Jesus like a cornerstone?

How can Jesus be a foundation for you?

You are here

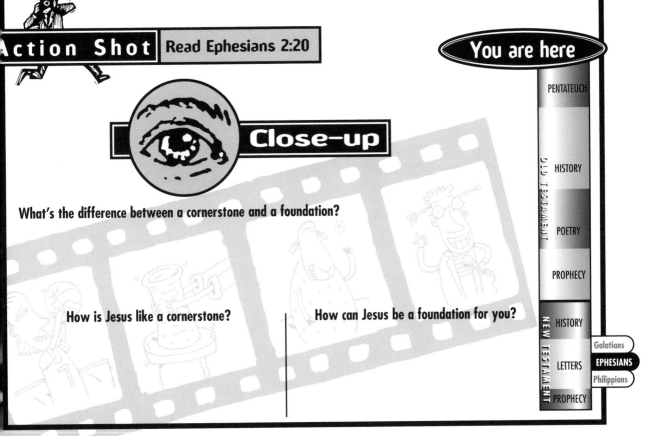

OLD TESTAMENT
PENTATEUCH
HISTORY
POETRY
PROPHECY

NEW TESTAMENT
HISTORY
LETTERS
PROPHECY

Galatians
EPHESIANS
Philippians

Self-portrait

Only Jesus can be the cornerstone in life. You can't be one for someone else or his life will be as off balance as the Leaning Tower of Pisa. But what does a cornerstone *do*? (More than one might be right.)

a. provides a firm foundation
b. sets a direction

c. holds important documents and papers
d. provides a reference for how things should be

Which of those things could you do for other people? (Circle the letters.)

Tell about a time you did one of those things. What was the result?

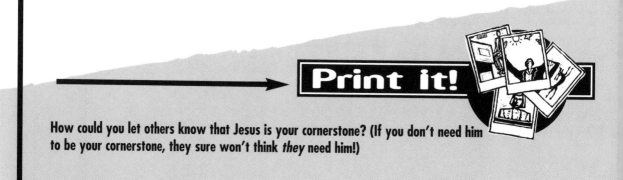

Print it!

How could you let others know that Jesus is your cornerstone? (If you don't need him to be your cornerstone, they sure won't think *they* need him!)

Who will you tell this to in the next few days? How will you do it?

God is like a MESSENGER

Then suddenly the Lord you are seeking will come to his temple; the messenger of the covenant, whom you desire, will come. Malachi 3:1

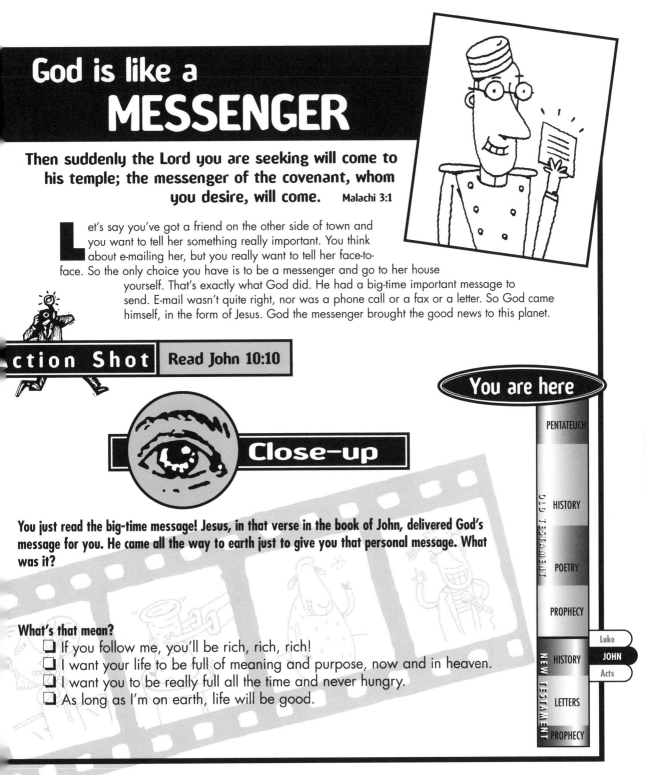

Let's say you've got a friend on the other side of town and you want to tell her something really important. You think about e-mailing her, but you really want to tell her face-to-face. So the only choice you have is to be a messenger and go to her house yourself. That's exactly what God did. He had a big-time important message to send. E-mail wasn't quite right, nor was a phone call or a fax or a letter. So God came himself, in the form of Jesus. God the messenger brought the good news to this planet.

Action Shot — Read John 10:10

Close-up

You are here

PENTATEUCH

OLD TESTAMENT

HISTORY

POETRY

PROPHECY

Luke
JOHN
Acts

NEW TESTAMENT

HISTORY

LETTERS

PROPHECY

You just read the big-time message! Jesus, in that verse in the book of John, delivered God's message for you. He came all the way to earth just to give you that personal message. What was it?

What's that mean?
- ☐ If you follow me, you'll be rich, rich, rich!
- ☐ I want your life to be full of meaning and purpose, now and in heaven.
- ☐ I want you to be really full all the time and never hungry.
- ☐ As long as I'm on earth, life will be good.

Write a few words that describe the kind of messenger Jesus was (like *loving* or *honest*—and no fair using those two words now!).

You can deliver all kinds of messages, good and bad. Circle the messages you've delivered in the last few months.

GOOD NEWS

truth

God-news

mean put-downs

hate   SHAME

useless information

gossip

bad news   fun   compliments   hope

Write about a time you were a good or helpful messenger.

Write about a time you were a bad or destructive messenger.

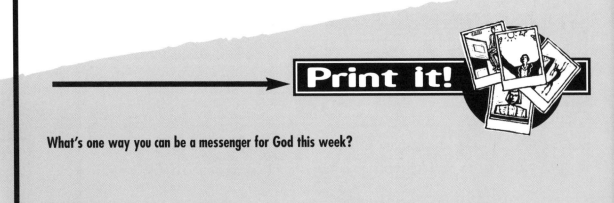

Print it!

What's one way you can be a messenger for God this week?

God is like a
FIRE

For our God is a consuming fire.   Hebrews 12:29

Yep, God is like a fire. He warms you and lights up your darkest places. When he thaws out your heart, you begin feeling things inside you that you didn't know were there. If you move too far away from him, you feel cold and alone. Get real close again, and you feel like a friend of his instead of like an enemy. You could melt just by seeing his face.

ction Shot   Read Psalm 83:14–15

You are here

Close-up

What are the things fire does? (Check all that apply.)
- ❑ gives light
- ❑ rides mopeds
- ❑ burns
- ❑ cooks things
- ❑ destroys things
- ❑ provides warmth
- ❑ cans jellies
- ❑ lights things

You should have checked all but two of 'em. Now go back over the list and circle the things God does.

Circle the sentence you think is most true.

- God is like fire because he warms up my life.

- God is like fire because he gives light where there's darkness.

- God is like fire because his anger can torch things.

- God is like fire because he gives warmth and light, but he's kinda dangerous, too.

PENTATEUCH

OLD TESTAMENT

HISTORY

Job

PSALMS

Proverbs

POETRY

PROPHECY

NEW TESTAMENT

HISTORY

LETTERS

PROPHECY

Rate the fieriness of Cora and Gunnar. Write a big 1 *(toasty!)*, **2** *(flicker)*, **or 3** *(cold ashes)* **on top of their stories.**

Cora just found out that her friend gets beaten all the time by her stepfather. The situation seems so dark, but Cora tries to help, even a little bit, by writing her friend a little encouraging note every day.

The camp speaker talked about giving Jesus control of every area of your life. Gunnar realized that he had a bunch of junk in his life that would displease Jesus, so he made a decision to get out his spiritual blowtorch.

How fiery are you? Circle one of these pictures to represent your answer.

Print it!

Think of someone who needs a bit of fire. What can you do about it?

God is like a
MOM

As a mother comforts her child, so will I comfort you.
Isaiah 66:13

Moms know how to comfort. It's just part of being a mom. Hot chocolate on a cold day. A Band-Aid placed just right over a boo-boo. The bedtime tuck and a kiss on the forehead. God does the same thing for us. When we're depressed, he listens and encourages. When we're hurt, he bundles us up and takes care of us. All the good things moms do—God does them, too.

Action Shot | **Read Psalm 119:76–77**

Close-up

You are here

What are the three most important responsibilities of a mom?

1.

2.

3.

Use the three letters in the word mom to write an acrostic about God's mom-like qualities.

M

O

M

PENTATEUCH

OLD TESTAMENT

HISTORY

Job
PSALMS
Proverbs

POETRY

PROPHECY

NEW TESTAMENT

HISTORY

LETTERS

PROPHECY

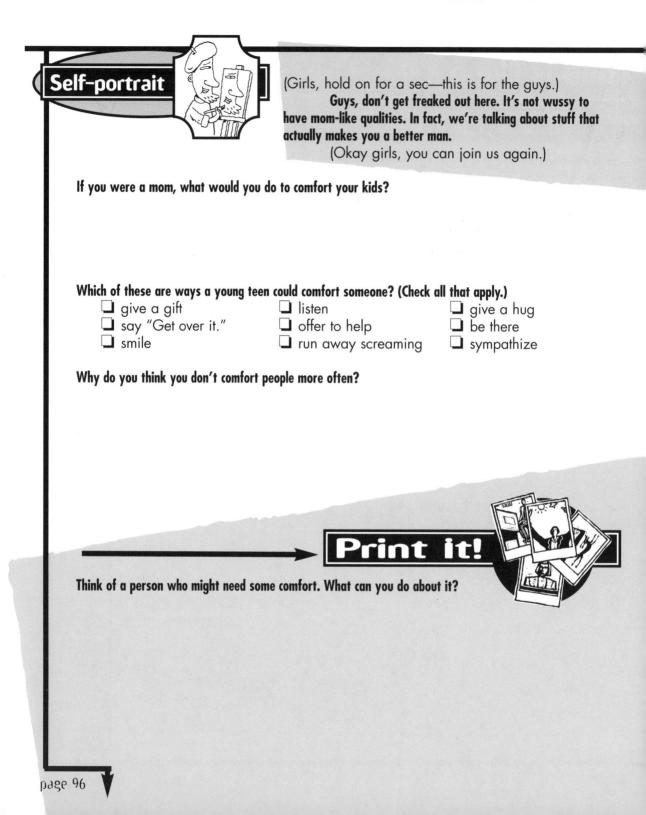

Self-portrait

(Girls, hold on for a sec—this is for the guys.)

Guys, don't get freaked out here. It's not wussy to have mom-like qualities. In fact, we're talking about stuff that actually makes you a better man.

(Okay girls, you can join us again.)

If you were a mom, what would you do to comfort your kids?

Which of these are ways a young teen could comfort someone? (Check all that apply.)

❑ give a gift
❑ say "Get over it."
❑ smile

❑ listen
❑ offer to help
❑ run away screaming

❑ give a hug
❑ be there
❑ sympathize

Why do you think you don't comfort people more often?

Print it!

Think of a person who might need some comfort. What can you do about it?

God is like a
RESCUE WORKER

For he has rescued us from the dominion of darkness and brought us into the kingdom of the Son he loves.
Colossians 1:13

A paramedic studies, trains, and rehearses long and hard for one job—to save lives. He saves babies, the elderly, friends, strangers, handsome people, ugly people, heroes, and criminals. It's his job. It's Jesus' job, too. He doesn't just save the rich or the good-looking or those with perfect church-attendance records. He saves anyone who calls for him.

Action Shot   Read Psalm 142:6

Close-up

What's the main thing that God rescues us from?

- ❏ stupidity
- ❏ mean people
- ❏ quizzes
- ❏ lime Jell-O
- ❏ hell
- ❏ rabid hamsters

What other things might he rescue you from?

Here's a business card for God the Rescue Worker. What else should it say?

God

YOU ARE HERE

PENTATEUCH

OLD TESTAMENT

HISTORY

Job

PSALMS

Proverbs

POETRY

PROPHECY

NEW TESTAMENT

HISTORY

LETTERS

PROPHECY

Crystal has a friend who's really depressed. She used to be fun, but now she's down all the time. Crystal has tried to reach out to her, but isn't sure what to do or say. How can she be a rescue worker for her friend?

Jason can tell his dad's a bit freaked out right now: he brings work home from the office every night, and it doesn't seem like he's getting much sleep. He's cranky and doesn't have time for anything fun. How can Jason be a rescue worker for his dad?

When have you been a rescue worker? What happened?

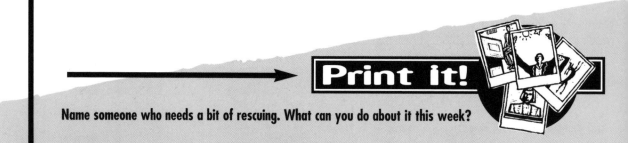

Print it!

Name someone who needs a bit of rescuing. What can you do about it this week?

God is like a
GUiDE

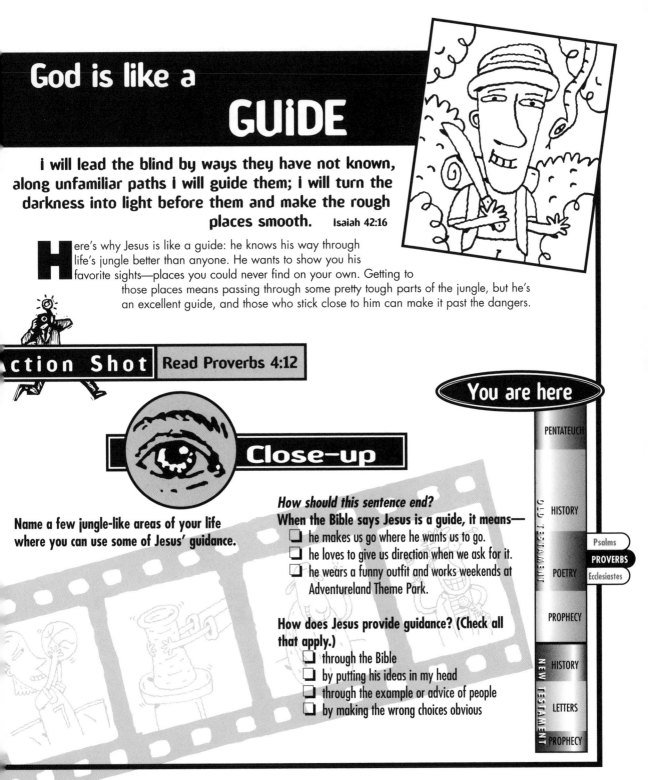

i will lead the blind by ways they have not known, along unfamiliar paths i will guide them; i will turn the darkness into light before them and make the rough places smooth. Isaiah 42:16

Here's why Jesus is like a guide: he knows his way through life's jungle better than anyone. He wants to show you his favorite sights—places you could never find on your own. Getting to those places means passing through some pretty tough parts of the jungle, but he's an excellent guide, and those who stick close to him can make it past the dangers.

ction Shot Read Proverbs 4:12

Close-up

Name a few jungle-like areas of your life where you can use some of Jesus' guidance.

How should this sentence end?
When the Bible says Jesus is a guide, it means—
- ❏ he makes us go where he wants us to go.
- ❏ he loves to give us direction when we ask for it.
- ❏ he wears a funny outfit and works weekends at Adventureland Theme Park.

How does Jesus provide guidance? (Check all that apply.)
- ❏ through the Bible
- ❏ by putting his ideas in my head
- ❏ through the example or advice of people
- ❏ by making the wrong choices obvious

You are here

PENTATEUCH

OLD TESTAMENT

HISTORY

Psalms
PROVERBS
Ecclesiastes

POETRY

PROPHECY

NEW TESTAMENT

HISTORY

LETTERS

PROPHECY

Underline the words you think fit best into this paragraph.

Sure, I'm not (Jesus / myself today / the tour guide at my school)**. So I'll never be as good a** (wrestler / guide / hall monitor) **as Jesus. But with his help I can** (help point people in the right direction / help point at things / point out the bathrooms to new kids at school). **I can help my friends see** (why I'm such a cool guide / dangers they should avoid / the best route to their third period class). **And I can show them by the way I live that** (Jesus provides the only real solutions in life / I'm better than they are / I dig my school).

Write about a time when you provided guidance for someone.

Did she follow your guidance? What happened?

What's the best way to provide guidance for your friends? (Check one.)

❏ tell them   ❏ show them by the way I live
❏ write them a note   ❏ draw them a map

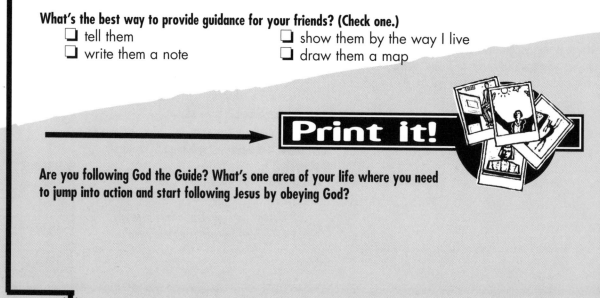

Print it!

Are you following God the Guide? What's one area of your life where you need to jump into action and start following Jesus by obeying God?

God is like a
BABY

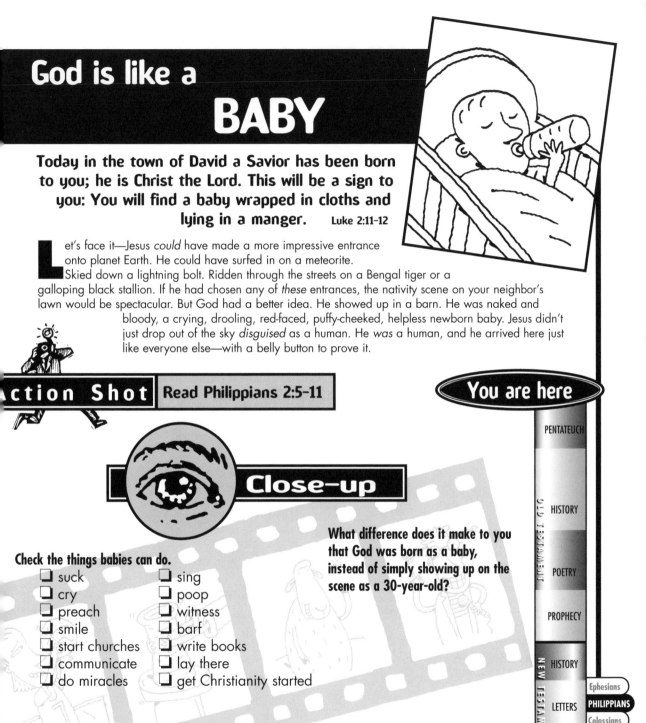

Today in the town of David a Savior has been born to you; he is Christ the Lord. This will be a sign to you: You will find a baby wrapped in cloths and lying in a manger. Luke 2:11-12

Let's face it—Jesus *could* have made a more impressive entrance onto planet Earth. He could have surfed in on a meteorite. Skied down a lightning bolt. Ridden through the streets on a Bengal tiger or a galloping black stallion. If he had chosen any of *these* entrances, the nativity scene on your neighbor's lawn would be spectacular. But God had a better idea. He showed up in a barn. He was naked and bloody, a crying, drooling, red-faced, puffy-cheeked, helpless newborn baby. Jesus didn't just drop out of the sky *disguised* as a human. He *was* a human, and he arrived here just like everyone else—with a belly button to prove it.

Action Shot — Read Philippians 2:5-11

Close-up

Check the things babies can do.

- suck
- cry
- preach
- smile
- start churches
- communicate
- do miracles
- sing
- poop
- witness
- barf
- write books
- lay there
- get Christianity started

What difference does it make to you that God was born as a baby, instead of simply showing up on the scene as a 30-year-old?

You are here

OLD TESTAMENT
- PENTATEUCH
- HISTORY
- POETRY
- PROPHECY

NEW TESTAMENT
- HISTORY
- LETTERS — Ephesians / **PHILIPPIANS** / Colossians
- PROPHECY

Self-portrait

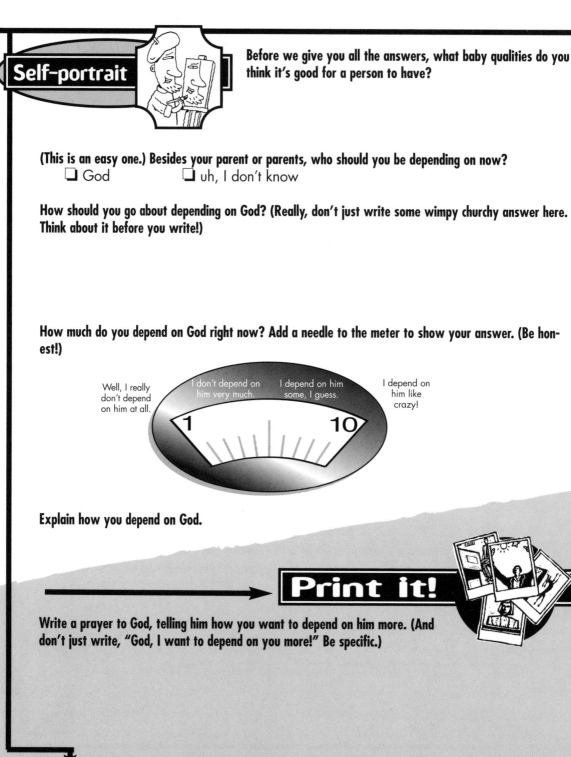

Before we give you all the answers, what baby qualities do you think it's good for a person to have?

(This is an easy one.) Besides your parent or parents, who should you be depending on now?

❏ God ❏ uh, I don't know

How should you go about depending on God? (Really, don't just write some wimpy churchy answer here. Think about it before you write!)

How much do you depend on God right now? Add a needle to the meter to show your answer. (Be honest!)

Well, I really don't depend on him at all.

I don't depend on him very much.

I depend on him some, I guess.

I depend on him like crazy!

1   10

Explain how you depend on God.

Print it!

Write a prayer to God, telling him how you want to depend on him more. (And don't just write, "God, I want to depend on you more!" Be specific.)

God is like a
KiNG

i am the Lord, your Holy One, israel's Creator, your King. Isaiah 43:15

You're pacing slowly up the aisle. Thousands of eyes are watching you. An organ is playing impressively formal music. When you get to the front, someone hands you a metal stick with gems all over it. Then they place a crown (with more gems) on your head. You're the new king! Whatever you say, goes. You want more chocolate? Here it is. You want a law that says no school on Mondays? Done. You want even *more* gems? They're yours. Kings have all the power. Whatever they say is the law. That's why our God is so amazing. He's the king (not the president or the prime minister), and he's an all-powerful ruler. But he's a kind, loving, fair, just, all-powerful ruler. And that's the best kind of king there is!

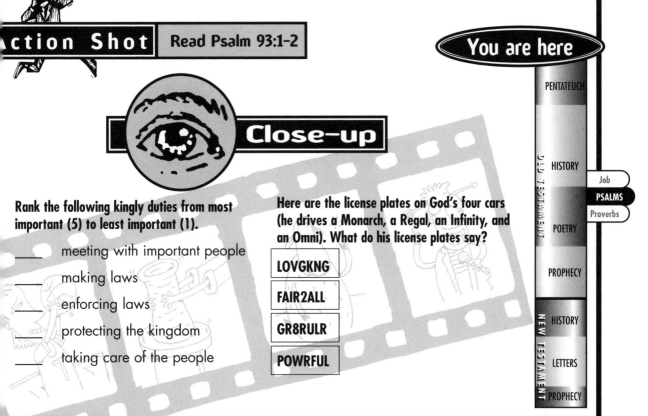

Action Shot | **Read Psalm 93:1-2**

Close-up

Rank the following kingly duties from most important (5) to least important (1).

____ meeting with important people

____ making laws

____ enforcing laws

____ protecting the kingdom

____ taking care of the people

Here are the license plates on God's four cars (he drives a Monarch, a Regal, an Infinity, and an Omni). What do his license plates say?

LOVGKNG

FAIR2ALL

GR8RULR

POWRFUL

You are here

PENTATEUCH

OLD TESTAMENT

HISTORY

Job
PSALMS
Proverbs

POETRY

PROPHECY

NEW TESTAMENT

HISTORY

LETTERS

PROPHECY

Self-portrait

If you were a new king, what would be your first action?

This is a tough one. God's a king because—well, because he's God. You and I may not be kings, but we can be *kingly*—in other words, we can still do things a king would do. What are some of those things?

What things have you been given responsibility for? (Check all that apply.)

❑ keeping my room livable   ❑ getting my homework done
❑ taking care of my siblings   ❑ doing chores
❑ taking care of a pet   ❑ spending and saving my money
❑ maintaining friendships   ❑ bathing and grooming myself

Okay, here's a very personal question. Of the things you just checked, how are you doing with these?

Print it!

What's a creative way you could be king-like in serving God?

God is like a HUMAN

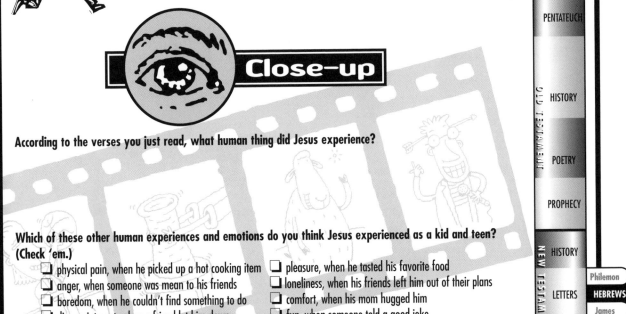

The Word became flesh and made his dwelling among us. John 1:14

Ever had an ant farm? You know, those thin, clear-sided things that let you watch the ants build their maze of tunnels? Imagine for a minute that you could join your ants on the farm for a few days—not as a mini-version of your human self, but as an ant. Pure ant—segmented body, exoskeleton, and all. Chances are, once you came back to the human world, you'd understand what it's like to be an ant—their ant-troubles, ant-joys, ant-fears. All their little six-legged emotions.

That's what Jesus did (but for 33 years). By leaving heaven and living on earth as a human, he did more than offer you salvation: he experienced feelings just like yours, fears just like yours, frustrations just like yours. Human through and through, just like you. (In addition to being all-human, Jesus was also all-God—but that's another story.)

Action Shot | Read Hebrews 4:15–16

Close-up

According to the verses you just read, what human thing did Jesus experience?

Which of these other human experiences and emotions do you think Jesus experienced as a kid and teen? (Check 'em.)

- ☐ physical pain, when he picked up a hot cooking item
- ☐ anger, when someone was mean to his friends
- ☐ boredom, when he couldn't find something to do
- ☐ disappointment, when a friend let him down
- ☐ sleepiness, when he just couldn't keep his eyes open
- ☐ pleasure, when he tasted his favorite food
- ☐ loneliness, when his friends left him out of their plans
- ☐ comfort, when his mom hugged him
- ☐ fun, when someone told a good joke
- ☐ temptation, when he wanted something he couldn't have

You are here

PENTATEUCH

OLD TESTAMENT
HISTORY

POETRY

PROPHECY

NEW TESTAMENT
HISTORY

LETTERS

PROPHECY

Philemon
HEBREWS
James

What difference does it make to you that Jesus experienced all these things?
- ❏ the next answer
- ❏ it means that he really understands when I feel those things, just like the ant farm example given earlier
- ❏ the answer above this one
- ❏ all of the above

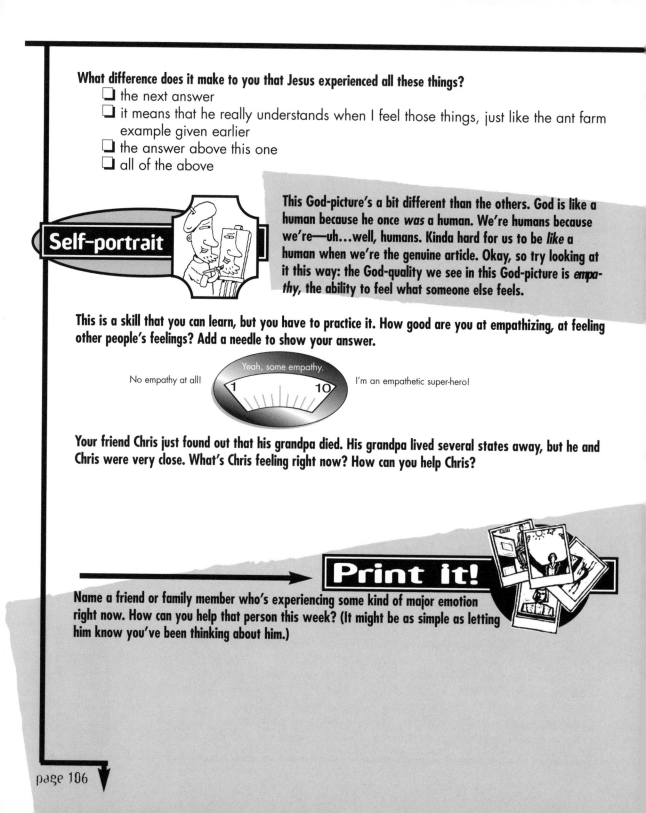

Self-portrait

This God-picture's a bit different than the others. God is like a human because he once *was* a human. We're humans because we're—uh...well, humans. Kinda hard for us to be *like* a human when we're the genuine article. Okay, so try looking at it this way: the God-quality we see in this God-picture is *empathy*, the ability to feel what someone else feels.

This is a skill that you can learn, but you have to practice it. How good are you at empathizing, at feeling other people's feelings? Add a needle to show your answer.

No empathy at all!   Yeah, some empathy.   I'm an empathetic super-hero!
1   10

Your friend Chris just found out that his grandpa died. His grandpa lived several states away, but he and Chris were very close. What's Chris feeling right now? How can you help Chris?

Print it!

Name a friend or family member who's experiencing some kind of major emotion right now. How can you help that person this week? (It might be as simple as letting him know you've been thinking about him.)

God is like a
LISTENER

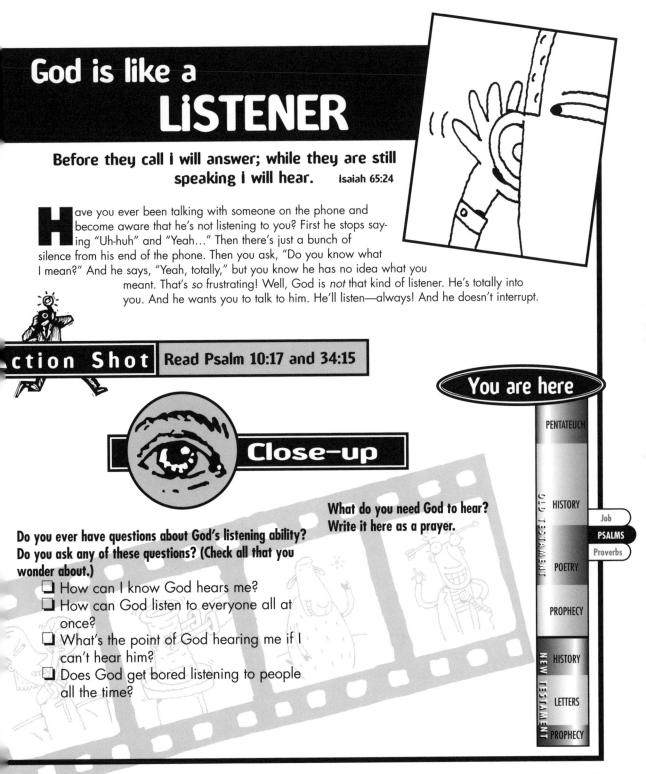

Before they call I will answer; while they are still speaking I will hear. Isaiah 65:24

Have you ever been talking with someone on the phone and become aware that he's not listening to you? First he stops saying "Uh-huh" and "Yeah..." Then there's just a bunch of silence from his end of the phone. Then you ask, "Do you know what I mean?" And he says, "Yeah, totally," but you know he has no idea what you meant. That's *so* frustrating! Well, God is *not* that kind of listener. He's totally into you. And he wants you to talk to him. He'll listen—always! And he doesn't interrupt.

ction Shot Read Psalm 10:17 and 34:15

Close-up

Do you ever have questions about God's listening ability? Do you ask any of these questions? (Check all that you wonder about.)

❑ How can I know God hears me?
❑ How can God listen to everyone all at once?
❑ What's the point of God hearing me if I can't hear him?
❑ Does God get bored listening to people all the time?

What do you need God to hear? Write it here as a prayer.

You are here

PENTATEUCH

OLD TESTAMENT

HISTORY

POETRY

PROPHECY

NEW TESTAMENT

HISTORY

LETTERS

PROPHECY

Job
PSALMS
Proverbs

Self-portrait

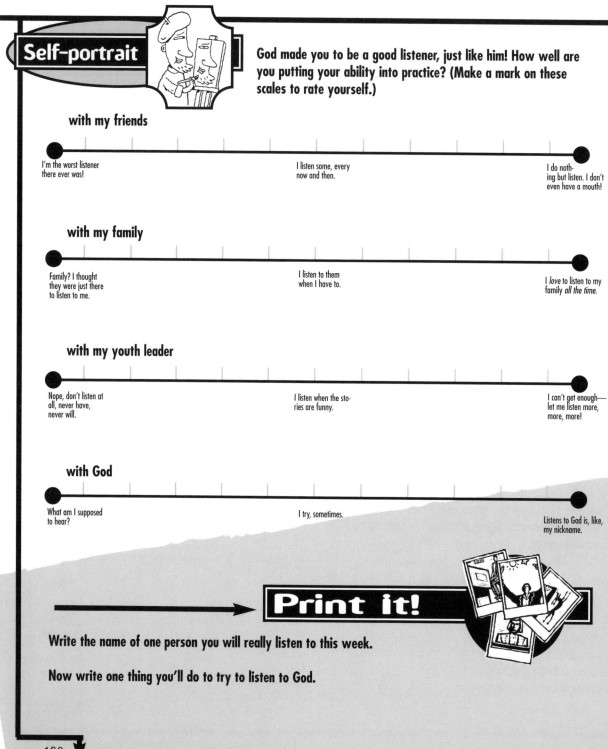

God made you to be a good listener, just like him! How well are you putting your ability into practice? (Make a mark on these scales to rate yourself.)

with my friends

I'm the worst listener there ever was!

I listen some, every now and then.

I do nothing but listen. I don't even have a mouth!

with my family

Family? I thought they were just there to listen to me.

I listen to them when I have to.

I *love* to listen to my family *all the time.*

with my youth leader

Nope, don't listen at all, never have, never will.

I listen when the stories are funny.

I can't get enough—let me listen more, more, more!

with God

What am I supposed to hear?

I try, sometimes.

Listens to God is, like, my nickname.

Print it!

Write the name of one person you will really listen to this week.

Now write one thing you'll do to try to listen to God.

Resources from Youth Specialties

Professional Resources

Administration, Publicity, & Fundraising (Ideas Library)

Developing Student Leaders

Equipped to Serve: Volunteer Youth Worker Training Course

Help! I'm a Junior High Youth Worker!

Help! I'm a Small-Group Leader!

Help! I'm a Sunday School Teacher!

Help! I'm a Volunteer Youth Worker!

How to Expand Your Youth Ministry

How to Speak to Youth...and Keep Them Awake at the Same Time

Junior High Ministry (Updated & Expanded)

The Ministry of Nurture: A Youth Worker's Guide to Discipling Teenagers

One Kid at a Time: Reaching Youth through Mentoring

Purpose-Driven Youth Ministry

Purpose-Driven Youth Ministry Video Curriculum

So That's Why I Keep Doing This! 52 Devotional Stories for Youth Workers

A Youth Ministry Crash Course

The Youth Worker's Handbook to Family Ministry

Youth Ministry Programming

Camps, Retreats, Missions, & Service Ideas (Ideas Library)

Compassionate Kids: Practical Ways to Involve Your Students in Mission and Service

Creative Bible Lessons from the Old Testament

Creative Bible Lessons in 1 & 2 Corinthians

Creative Bible Lessons in John: Encounters with Jesus

Creative Bible Lessons in Romans: Faith on Fire!

Creative Bible Lessons on the Life of Christ

Creative Junior High Programs from A to Z, Vol. 1 (A-M)

Creative Junior High Programs from A to Z, Vol. 2 (N-Z)

Creative Meetings, Bible Lessons, & Worship Ideas (Ideas Library)

Crowd Breakers & Mixers (Ideas Library)

Drama, Skits, & Sketches (Ideas Library)

Drama, Skits, & Sketches 2 (Ideas Library)

Dramatic Pauses

Everyday Object Lessons

Facing Your Future: Graduating Youth Group with a Faith That Lasts

Games (Ideas Library)

Games 2 (Ideas Library)

Great Fundraising Ideas for Youth Groups

More Great Fundraising Ideas for Youth Groups

Great Retreats for Youth Groups

Greatest Skits on Earth

Greatest Skits on Earth, Vol. 2

Holiday Ideas (Ideas Library)

Hot Illustrations for Youth Talks

More Hot Illustrations for Youth Talks

Still More Hot Illustrations for Youth Talks

Incredible Questionnaires for Youth Ministry

Junior High Game Nights

More Junior High Game Nights

Kickstarters: 101 Ingenious Intros to Just about Any Bible Lesson

Live the Life! Student Evangelism Training Kit

Memory Makers

Play It! Great Games for Groups

Play It Again! More Great Games for Groups

Special Events (Ideas Library)

Spontaneous Melodramas

Super Sketches for Youth Ministry

(more on next page)

(continued from previous page)

Teaching the Bible Creatively
Videos That Teach
What Would Jesus Do? Youth Leader's Kit
WWJD—The Next Level
Wild Truth Bible Lessons
Wild Truth Bible Lessons 2
Wild Truth Bible Lessons—Pictures of God
Worship Services for Youth Groups

Discussion Starters

Discussion & Lesson Starters (Ideas Library)
Discussion & Lesson Starters 2 (Ideas Library)
Get 'Em Talking
Keep 'Em Talking!
High School TalkSheets
More High School TalkSheets
High School TalkSheets: Psalms and Proverbs
Junior High TalkSheets
More Junior High TalkSheets
Junior High TalkSheets: Psalms and Proverbs
What If...? 450 Thought-Provoking Questions to
    Get Teenagers Talking, Laughing, and Thinking
Would You Rather...? 465 Provocative Questions to
    Get Teenagers Talking
Have You Ever...? 450 Intriguing Questions
    Guaranteed to Get Teenagers Talking

Clip Art

ArtSource: Stark Raving Clip Art (print)
ArtSource: Youth Group Activities (print)
ArtSource CD-ROM: Ultimate Clip Art
ArtSource CD-ROM: Clip Art Library Version 2.0

Videos

EdgeTV
The Heart of Youth Ministry: A Morning with Mike
    Yaconelli
Next Time I Fall in Love Video Curriculum
Understanding Your Teenager Video Curriculum

Student Books

Grow For It Journal
Grow For It Journal through the Scriptures
Teen Devotional Bible
What Would Jesus Do? Spiritual Challenge Journal
WWJD Spiritual Challenge Journal: The Next Level
Wild Truth Journal for Junior Highers
Wild Truth Journal—Pictures of God